IMAGES of America
ARTHURDALE

To Craig —

A Fenix

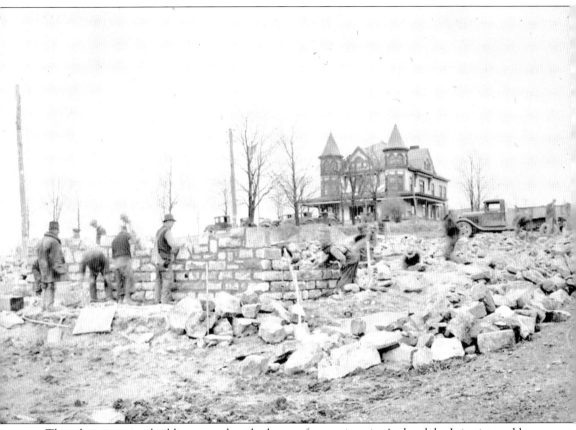

The administration building served as the heart of operations in Arthurdale. It is pictured here under construction with the Arthur Mansion in the background. Federal offices were located in the administration building, where homesteaders would pay their rent and speak with the project manager. Arthurdale Heritage, Inc., restored the building in the late 1980s and early 1990s, and it now serves as part of the New Deal Homestead Museum. (Courtesy West Virginia and Regional History Collection [WVRHC].)

ON THE COVER: West Virginia representative Jennings Randolph (fourth from left) poses with project manager Bushrod Grimes (second from right) and landscape architect John Nolan (third from right), among others, in front of the Arthur Mansion. Randolph was elected in 1933 and served seven terms in the House of Representatives before being elected to the U.S. Senate for five terms. This photograph was taken c. 1933. (Courtesy WVRHC.)

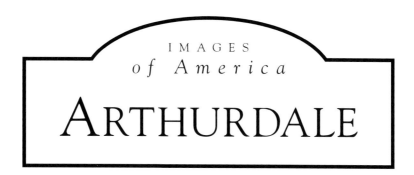

IMAGES of America

ARTHURDALE

Amanda Griffith Penix
on behalf of Arthurdale Heritage, Inc.

Copyright © 2007 by Amanda Griffith Penix on behalf of Arthurdale Heritage, Inc.
ISBN 978-0-7385-4433-5

Published by Arcadia Publishing
Charleston SC, Chicago IL, Portsmouth NH, San Francisco CA

Printed in the United States of America

Library of Congress Catalog Card Number: 2006940474

For all general information contact Arcadia Publishing at:
Telephone 843-853-2070
Fax 843-853-0044
E-mail sales@arcadiapublishing.com
For customer service and orders:
Toll-Free 1-888-313-2665

Visit us on the Internet at www.arcadiapublishing.com

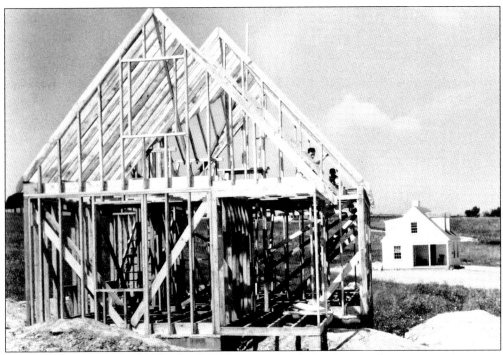

During 1935 and 1944, the federal government spearheaded a photography project to document Resettlement Administration projects, including the construction of planned communities like Arthurdale. The project employed photographers such as Walker Evans, Elmer Johnson, Edwin Locke, Arthur Rothestein, Ben Shahan, and Marion Post Wolcott, whose work is shown in this book. The scope of the project expanded to document sharecroppers in the South, migratory agricultural workers in the Midwest and West, and even mobilization efforts for World War II. The Farm Security Administration/Office of War Intelligence Photograph Collection consists of approximately 279,610 images and has been housed at the Library of Congress since 1944. (Courtesy Library of Congress.)

Contents

Acknowledgments		6
Introduction		7
1.	Scotts Run	9
2.	Back to the Land	23
3.	A New World	37
4.	Learning by Living	51
5.	A Cooperative Community	59
6.	Industrial Development	79
7.	A Community School	87
8.	Eleanor's Little Village	109
9.	The Dream Lives On	117

Acknowledgments

First and foremost, I would like to recognize the historians before me who have dedicated countless hours to researching the individual stories of Arthurdale and the New Deal. I relied on the respective works of Dr. Stephen Haid, Dr. Ronald Lewis, Jeanne Rymer, Dr. Sam Stack, and Dr. Jerry Bruce Thomas to form the basis of this book.

Over 20 years ago, the founding fathers and mothers of Arthurdale Heritage, Inc., paved the way for this book. Without their foresight, Arthurdale and its buildings would only be located in the history books instead of the living-history community into which it has developed. I would also like to give a special thank-you to the hundreds upon hundreds of Arthurdale Heritage volunteers who have worked to keep the Arthurdale Dream alive. I would also like to thank the Board of Directors of Arthurdale Heritage, Inc., for supporting the undertaking of projects such as this one. Special thanks go to Marilee Hall for her years of continued dedication to the organization.

I am grateful that I was afforded the wonderful opportunity to meet Glenna Williams, Arthurdale Heritage's first president. Her unwavering spirit and contagious desire to preserve the Arthurdale Dream served as great motivation for Arthurdale Heritage volunteers and continues to be a source of inspiration. May she live on in our memories as Arthurdale will in history books.

Photographs without credits are part of Arthurdale Heritage's archives, which is composed of generous donations from homesteaders, descendants, relatives, and residents of Arthurdale. Thank you for sharing a part of your history with us. I am also grateful for the help of Lori Hostuttler of the West Virginia and Regional History Collection at West Virginia University (WVRHC) and Trista Powell of the Special Collections Research Center (SCRC), Morris Library at Southern Illinois University Carbondale from which I used photographs from the Elsie Ripley Clapp Collection. Photographs credited to the Library of Congress are from the Farm Security Administration/Office of War Information Collection of the Prints and Photographs Division.

Finally, I am thankful to my family for fostering my interest in local history. I do not know many other families that take a tour of the Southern West Virginia coalfields for a family vacation, but I am forever grateful for those experiences. Most importantly, I wish to thank my husband, Mike, for his continued love and encouragement.

INTRODUCTION

I came to know the community of Arthurdale after graduating from West Virginia University (WVU) in 2003. A friend sent me an e-mail with the executive-director job posting for Arthurdale Heritage, Inc. The position sounded interesting, yet I was more intrigued about this nationally significant community that I knew relatively nothing about. I grew up only 100 miles from Arthurdale, and my father drove my family practically across the state and back on family trips more times that I can count. Still, I had no recollection of the community as a result of these educational expeditions across the Mountain State. What made me even more perplexed was the fact that I had just received my master's degree in history with a focus on West Virginia and Appalachian regional history from WVU and had merely touched on the topic of Arthurdale in my studies. So when I went to interview for the director's job, I was at a loss for words when the board of directors asked me what I could tell a kindergarten student about Arthurdale. Three years later, I could talk about "Eleanor's Little Village" for as long as you would like to.

As director of Arthurdale Heritage, Inc., I am faced with the goal of promoting Arthurdale and educating the public about this nationally significant community. My previous lack of knowledge about Arthurdale is what motivates me to do projects like this, educating more people about this unique community and West Virginia's 20th-century history, a subject that is often overlooked in our classrooms.

Beginning in 1880, the coal and timber industries arrived in agricultural West Virginia. Enticed by unregulated exploitation of natural resources, out-of-state companies brought welcomed employment; however, they also stripped the mountains of the virgin timber located over two-thirds of the state and robbed the coal from underneath them. Industrial development also brought with it the creation of new transportation networks, linking previously remote areas of the state with national markets. The timber industry enjoyed a short-lived reign, which was basically over by 1920. Mills soon closed, and railroads pulled up tracks. On the other hand, the coal industry saw a rapid growth in the first decade of the 20th century. World War I created a high demand for coal to fuel the fight for democracy around the world, resulting in numerous mines opening and in ample employment throughout the state. In the immediate post-war period, the coal industry entered into a prolonged decline, when production began to exceed demand. Although saturated with too many mines and miners, the coal industry continued to overproduce, lessening coal's market price and causing widespread unemployment during the 1920s. The downturn of the coal and timber industries combined with the decline of farm prices left West Virginians with little options when it came to employment in the early 1930s.

After Black Thursday on October 24, 1929, the Great Depression began causing rampant unemployment and homelessness throughout the United States. In 1933, Franklin D. Roosevelt took office as the nation's 32nd president. In his first 100 days, FDR created numerous "alphabet agencies" to promote the three components of his New Deal legislation: direct relief, economic recovery, and financial reform. In 1933, Congress passed the National Industrial Recovery Act (NIRA) to regulate businesses and create employment. Section 208 of Title II of the NIRA provided $25 million to fund the creation of subsistence homesteads.

Although the homestead-community program was one of the smallest New Deal programs, it was one of the most significant. The program would eventually build a total of 100 communities across the country to aid the poverty-stricken citizens of the United States. Arthurdale, the first of these New Deal Homestead Communities, became a pet project of First Lady Eleanor Roosevelt, who took great interest in its development after a visit to the coalfields of north central West Virginia in August 1933. Construction began on Arthurdale in the fall of that year, and the first 50 homesteaders had moved into their new homes by the summer of 1934. The federal government built 165 homes for the community along with community buildings, craft and industrial centers, and state-of-the-art schools.

In total, five agencies administered the New Deal community program throughout its lifetime: the Division of Subsistence Homesteads (1933–1935), the Federal Emergency Relief Administration (1933–1935), the Resettlement Administration (1935–1937), the Farm Security Administration (1937–942), and the Federal Public Housing Authority (1942–1947). The five agencies created 99 assorted communities. There were farming and industrial communities as well as African American and Jewish communities. The most famous of the New Deal communities are the "Green Towns" of Greenbelt, Maryland; Green Hills, Ohio; and Greendale, Wisconsin, whose original community designs are still considered among the most ambitious and creative public housing in the history of the country. Communities were built from New Jersey to Florida, North Carolina to California, and in most states in between.

The New Deal community program proved to be a great social experiment in the early 1930s. The Great Depression forced Americans to seek change, and the community program offered a way to lead the country into a new era. After five years of scrutiny and controversy, by 1937, the nation began to turn from the experimental New Deal programs to seek the more established, previous ways of thinking. Congress cut funding for the community program, which was seen as a nonessential program. By 1947, the federal government had officially sold all of its holdings in Arthurdale, and the nation's first homestead-community experiment ended.

Although not a financial success, the homestead project provided a new start in life for thousands of Americans during the Great Depression. First Lady Eleanor Roosevelt saw the success of the program not in monetary gains, but in the successful families it created. On a trip to Arthurdale in 1934, she visited a home in which she saw three young girls, ages 6, 8, and 10. The first lady was amazed that all three were of similar size and wondered if their previous living conditions in the coal mining camps had something to do with the underdevelopment of the older children. However, she noted that all three girls "looked rosy and healthy and supremely happy now!"

Decades of scrutiny have marked the New Deal homestead program as a failed federal program. Too often, the overrun budgets, botched construction, and socialistic qualities of the program overshadow the cottage craft industry, the cooperative community activities, and the homesteaders themselves. To the families who moved to the community, Arthurdale cannot be considered a failure. It provided them with not only a new home, but also a new lease on their lives, which would never be the same after moving to Arthurdale.

One

SCOTTS RUN

Located in Monongalia County, Scotts Run is a five-mile long hollow named after the winding stream that flows through the communities of Cassville, Jere, Pursglove, and Osage as it makes its way to the Monongahela River. Industrial development came in the late 19th century, and by World War I, Scotts Run was one of the most intensively developed coal districts in the United States. However, the economic downfall of the 1930s caused many of the coal mines in Scotts Run, and throughout Appalachia, to close or to operate sporadically. Coal miners, like the millions of unemployed Americans during the Great Depression, struggled to provide food and shelter for their families. It was at this time in Scotts Run history that it became the poster child of American poverty.

Lorena Hickok wrote that Scotts Run was the worst place she had ever seen with housing "most Americans would not have considered fit for pigs." Hickok came to north central West Virginia in 1933 as part of a tour to inspect the effects of the Depression on the Appalachian coalfields. An Associated Press reporter, Hickok was also one of Eleanor Roosevelt's closest friends. After hearing "Hick's" stories of Scotts Run, the first lady promptly left Washington, D.C., to visit with the impoverished coal miners and their families. Roosevelt traveled with Hickok, social worker Alice Davis, and Clarence Pickett, the executive secretary of the American Friends Service Committee. A Quaker organization founded in 1917, "the Friends" had been working in Scotts Run since 1931 to provide food, clothing, and work skills to miners and their families.

After her visit to Scotts Run, the first lady returned to Washington, D.C., with a newfound resolve to help its residents. Within two months, plans to create Arthurdale were well under way.

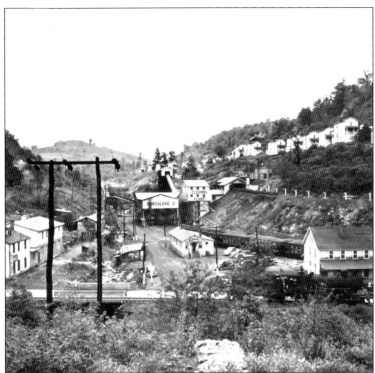

In 1880, agriculture dominated the Scotts Run area, with farmers making up over 60 percent of the population. However, by the mid-1920s, coal operations had sprung up along the hollow. By that time, miners made up 63 percent of the population and farming only represented 20 percent. (Courtesy Library of Congress.)

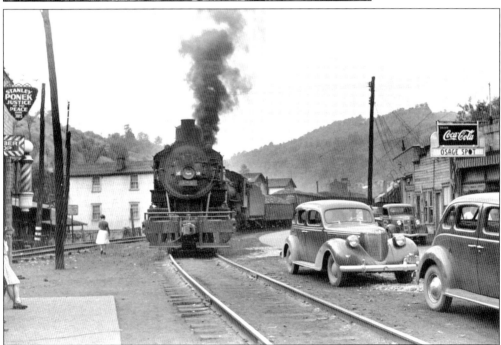

The coal trade publication *Black Diamond* proclaimed that no other coal district in West Virginia equaled the development in Scotts Run. Within seven years, coal tonnage produced in the hollow increased by 100 percent, reaching almost 4.4 million tons in 1921. Here a coal train pulls through the town of Osage. (Courtesy Library of Congress.)

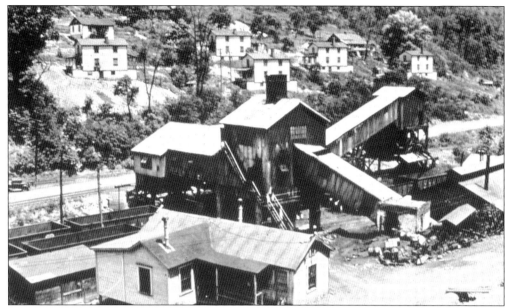

With the rapid industrial development in Scotts Run came a transformation of the hollow's landscape, including the appearance of coal tipples. Tipples served as the processing plant for the coal operations, where rock and shale were separated from the coal. Once separated, the coal would be shipped to various points around the country via the railroad or by river freight. (Courtesy WVRHC.)

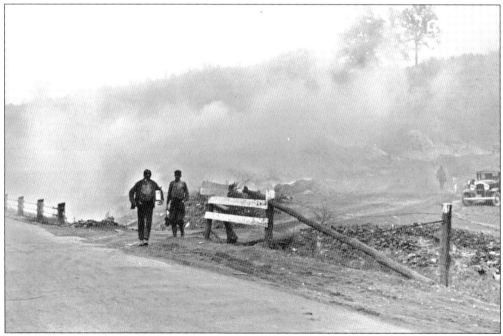

Slag piles were huge mountains created of rock and shale discarded from the tipple. Coal was still present in the mounds, so it was not unusual for them to catch on fire and burn continuously. Two Maidsville miners are pictured walking home from work with a slag heap burning behind them. (Courtesy Library of Congress.)

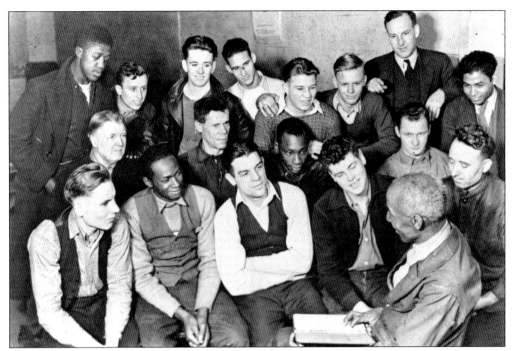

The changing landscape of Scotts Run also brought with it a changing social environment. Throughout the Appalachian coalfields, companies imported immigrants and African Americans from the South to work in the mines. By 1920, sixty percent of the population of Scotts Run was foreign born, with the remaining 40 percent made up of whites and African Americans equally. (Courtesy WVRHC.)

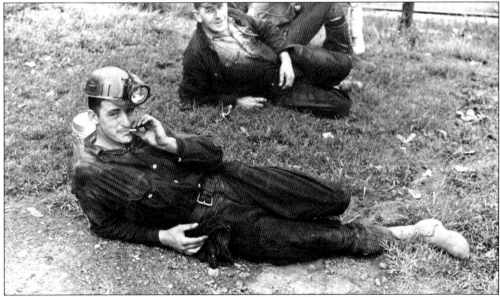

Hand loading coal was a tough job for miners. Using hand tools, the miner drilled holes into the seam of coal, filled the hole with powder, and blasted the wall of coal. He then loaded the broken coal into cars and was paid for the tonnage of coal he loaded. Here a Scotts Run coal miner takes a rest. (Courtesy Library of Congress.)

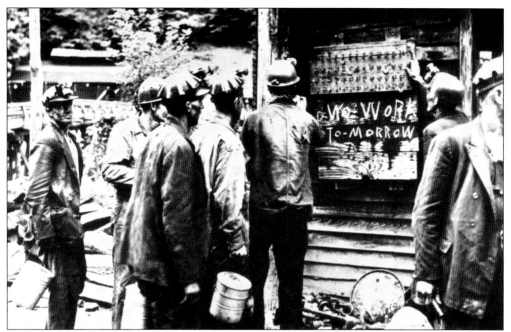

After World War I, the coal industry went into a decline due the development of alternative fuels and a reduction in demand. In 1922, the U.S. Coal Commission began a new mechanization program to replace hand loading in the mines. As a result of mechanization and the decline in demand for coal, thousands of miners began losing their jobs. (Courtesy WVRHC.)

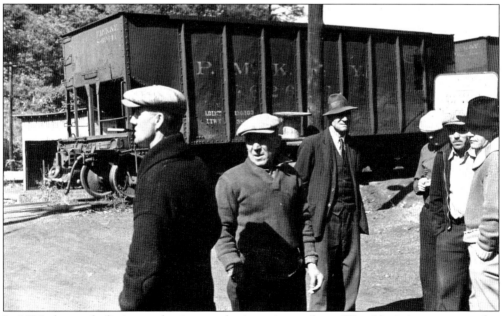

In 1924, due to declining coal prices, coal miners in northern West Virginia went on strike, marking the end of the prosperity in Scotts Run and the beginning of unequaled despair. The northern West Virginia mine war lasted until 1931, the longest strike in West Virginia history. The strike violence resulted in Scotts Run being nicknamed "Bloody Run." (Courtesy Library of Congress.)

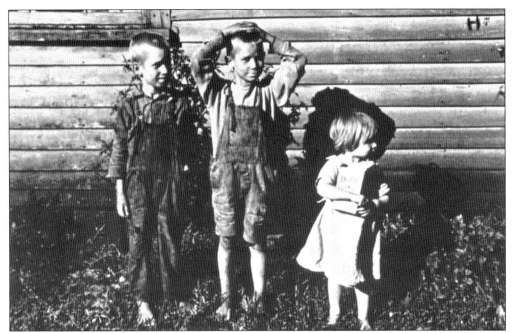

The emergence of the Great Depression added to the already deteriorating conditions in Scotts Run. Coal production in the county dropped significantly, and the American Friends Service Committee estimated that 200,000 miners were permanently out of work, while 300,000 worked only sporadically. Miners felt helpless when it came to providing for their families, who suffered from lack of food and proper shelter. (Courtesy Library of Congress.)

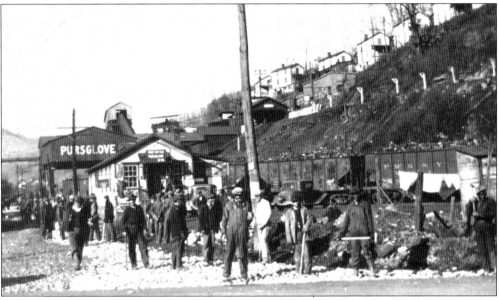

After his inauguration in 1933, Pres. Franklin D. Roosevelt began the New Deal programs that sought to give work to unemployed Americans. The Works Progress Administration (WPA) undertook road, sewer, and water projects throughout West Virginia and the nation. Here unemployed Scotts Run miners are shown constructing a road at the Pursglove No. 2 Mine through the WPA. (Courtesy WVRHC.)

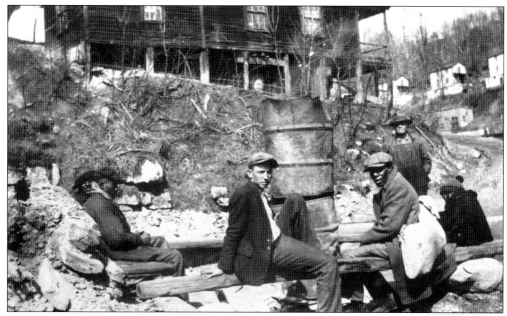

By 1928, the National Miners Union (NMU), shown at a picket line in 1933, began organizing Scotts Run miners to protest wage cuts and working conditions. Backed by the Communist Party, the NMU was not overly successful, but the Communist presence was enough to leave Eleanor Roosevelt with the opinion that a "people's revolution" could occur in Scotts Run. (Courtesy WVRHC.)

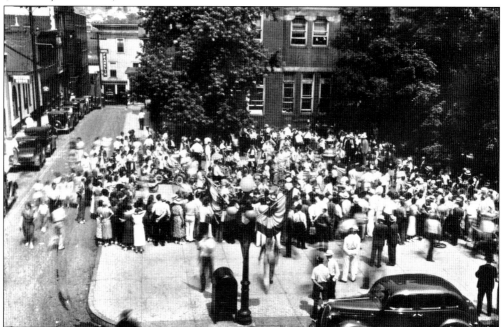

In October 1932, NMU organized Scotts Run miners to go out on a hunger strike, stating they could not work with their stomachs empty. The strike eventually ended after the miners marched from Pursglove to the Monongalia County Courthouse demanding food. The Monongalia County Courthouse Square is pictured with a crowd in 1933. (Courtesy WVRHC.)

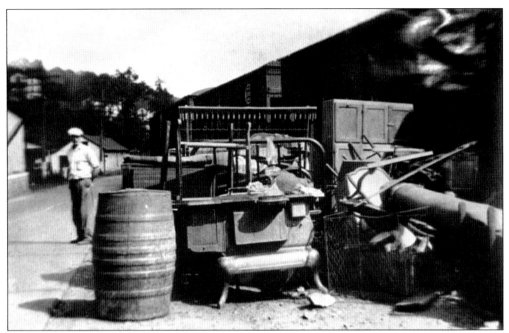

Because miners lived in company housing, coal operators often evicted striking miners from company property, pitching their belongings into the street. By law, companies had to give a 30-day notice prior to eviction; however, many forced families out of homes without warning, leaving miners to find shelter with friends and family or to live in tents. (Courtesy WVRHC.)

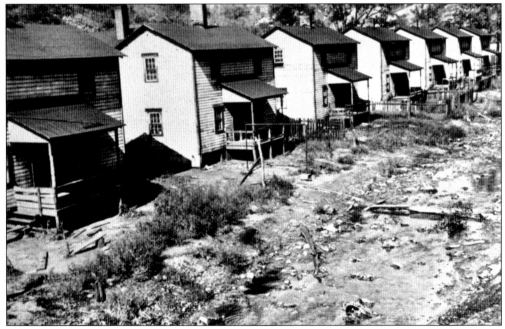

Pictured are the "ramshackled houses, black with coal dust" along Scotts Run that Lorena Hickok saw on her visit in the summer of 1933. Hickok lamented the fact that every night, the children who lived in those houses "went to sleep hungry, on piles of bug-infested rags spread on the floor." (Courtesy Library of Congress.)

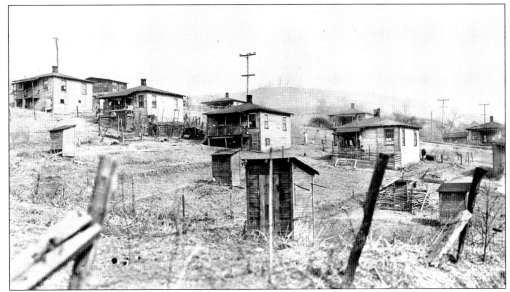

The company living conditions in Scotts Run were deplorable. Sewers and privies drained into the stream, from which everyone drew water. Eleanor Roosevelt said that the "filth was indescribable. You felt as though the coal dust had seeped into every crack in the house and it would be impossible to get them or the people clean." (Courtesy WVRHC.)

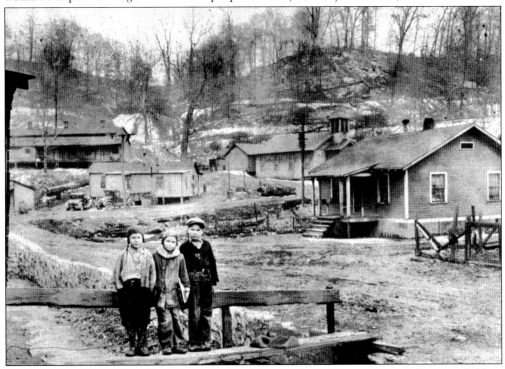

On her visit to Scotts Run, Elsie Clapp, Arthurdale school administrator, saw "[s]crawny children [that] played in the sulphur-stained puddles by the road and everywhere men and boys were standing about, not talking, just looking vacantly into space. Back from the highway, hundreds of black shanties rose tier on tier on the steep sides of the gulch." (Courtesy WVRHC.)

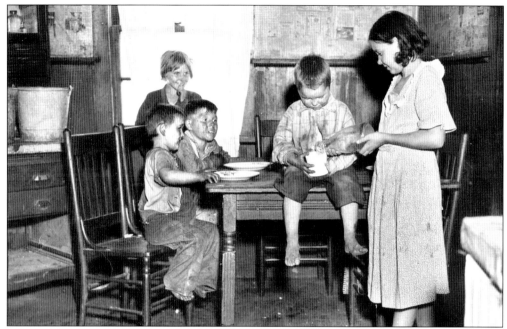

While in Scotts Run, Eleanor Roosevelt met an employed miner who showed her his weekly pay envelope. Inside was $1, on which he was to feed and clothe his children. In the miner's home, she "noticed a bowl on the table filled with scraps, the kind that you might give to a dog, and I saw children, evidently looking for their noon-day meal, take a handful out of that bowl and go out munching. That was all they had to eat." The meeting had a profound effect on the first lady, who used stories like this one to solicit donations from Washington socialites to help the starving families. (Courtesy Library of Congress.)

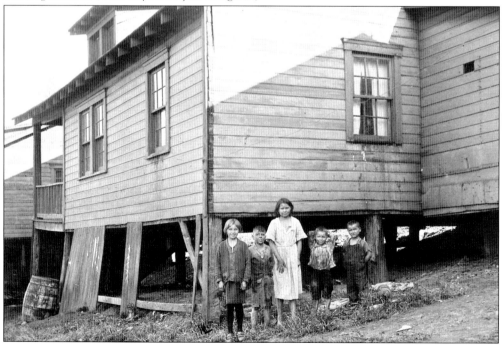

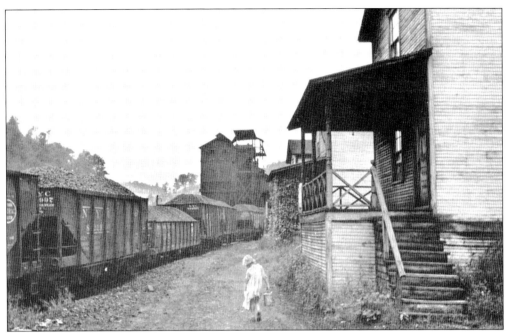

Eleanor Roosevelt brought a gentleman from New York City to Scotts Run, who, after seeing two sick children in one of the homes, came out and said, "I will give you any money you want to help remedy these conditions, but please do not ask me to go into any more houses. I feel contaminated and it makes me really ill." (Courtesy Library of Congress.)

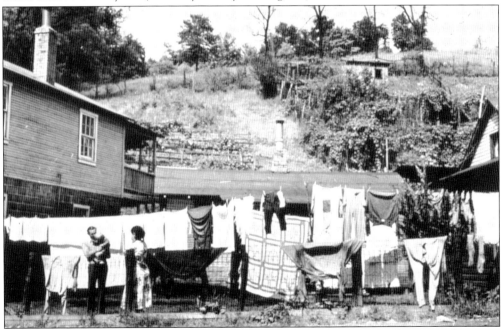

Glenna Williams, a future resident of Arthurdale, described her family's living conditions in Scotts Run as the depths of despair: "What can you do when there is nothing? We were on the brink of some kind of catastrophe. Our whole country was on the verge of disaster." (Courtesy Library of Congress.)

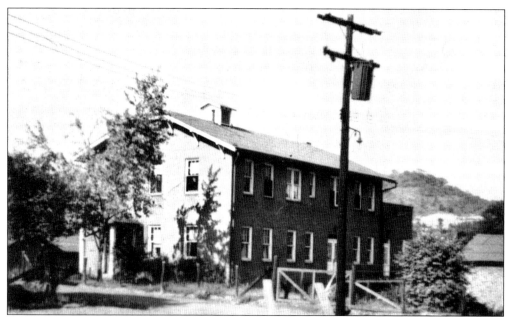

In 1922, the Women's Home Missionary Society of Wesley United Methodist Church began relief efforts in Scotts Run and established a Bible school for children. Programs at the Scotts Run Settlement House eventually included English literacy, citizenship, cooking, hygiene, and motherhood courses. The group built this permanent structure in 1927, and it still serves the area. (Courtesy WVRHC.)

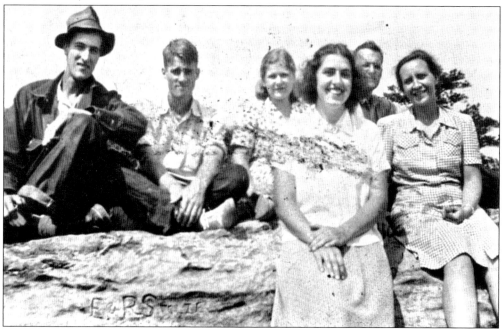

The American Friends Service Committee volunteers worked through a five-point program of rehabilitation: child feeding, health activities, cooperative shops, subsistence homestead leaders, and friendly counselors. In early 1932, with a budget of $250,000, the group fed as many as 40,000 children a day in 38 coalfield counties. (Courtesy WVRHC.)

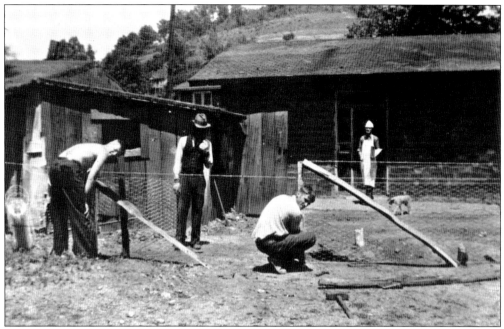

Comprised of doctors and dentists who worked for relatively no wages, the Council of Social Agencies supplemented the Friends, who distributed toothbrushes, towels, and soap to combat the remediable illnesses from which 95 percent of children in Monongalia County suffered. The Friends also undertook practical projects, including building fences and gardening. (Courtesy WVRHC.)

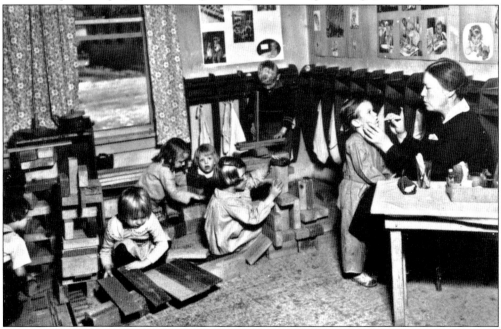

Clarence Pickett admitted that the success of the Friends was due to the dedication of Alice Davis and Nadia Danilevsky. The two women organized numerous programs, including clothing and food distribution, an outdoor community oven, a sewage system, and a nursery school in an abandoned company house. A Scotts Run nursery school is pictured. (Courtesy WVRHC.)

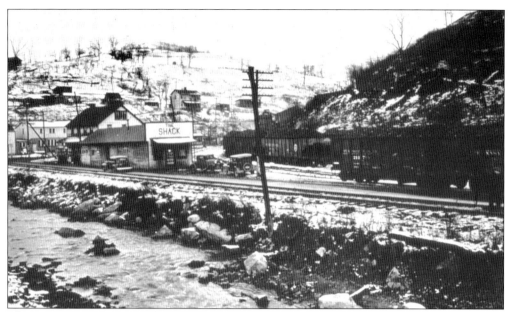

The Morgantown First Presbyterian Church began relief work in 1928, when Mary Behner, a member of the Student Volunteer Movement, came to Scotts Run to establish a missionary project that would Americanize immigrant coal miners. She also organized a library, a charm school for girls, and Sunday-school programs. Behner's efforts to find a home for her programs materialized in 1932, when the Pursglove Mining Company gave a former company store to house the project. Behner deemed the building "The Shack" and expanded programs to include a nursery school, a canning kitchen, mothers' clubs, nutrition classes, and a chef's club. Frank Trubee became the director of The Shack in 1938, built a larger building, and began cooperative exchanges of labor and goods based on the American Friends Service Committee philosophical approach. (Courtesy WVRHC.)

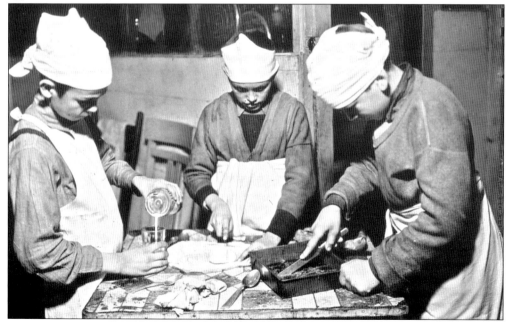

Two

BACK TO THE LAND

During the booming economy of the 1920s, millions of people left rural America to seek their fortunes in the cities. After the stock market crash of 1929, hundreds of thousands of disillusioned urbanites left the cities and headed back to the land. Articles in popular magazines urged readers to seek the economic and social independence offered by rural life.

Congress debated the subsistence homestead program as early as 1932 but did not take action on a federal program until Franklin D. Roosevelt's inauguration in 1933. As governor of New York, Roosevelt addressed rural relocation and had determined that proper infrastructure planning would improve rural life and encourage more migration from the cities to the country, restoring agriculture to economic equality with other industries. Congress set aside $25 million to fund a homestead-community program in the National Industrial Recovery Act of 1933. Milburn L. Wilson, director of the newly created Division of Subsistence Homesteads, believed that subsistence farming supplemented by industrial employment and training in handicrafts was the only effective way to operate the homestead-community program.

In the early 1930s, West Virginia University and the American Friends Service Committee were in the midst of planning a subsistence-garden program in Monongalia County. By June 1933, four hundred miners registered to be a part of the project, which was led by university employee Bushrod Grimes. When Eleanor Roosevelt visited Scotts Run in August 1933, Grimes informed her of the university's project, which greatly impressed the first lady. He inquired if property for the project could be purchased by the federal government. Within a week, Grimes and two other university faculty members began looking at possible sites for the project and soon settled on a tract of land located 14 miles from Morgantown in Preston County.

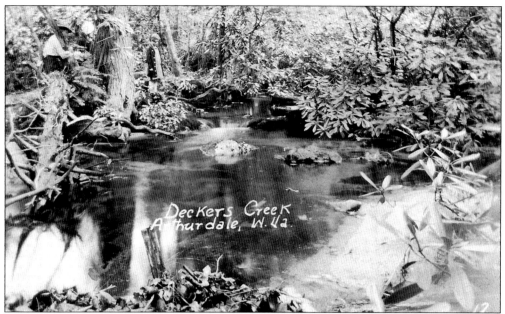

In 1789, John Fairfax purchased the Monongalia Glades from Philip Doddridge, one of Virginia's first congressmen elected from the western part of the state. Fairfax was a friend of George Washington, who had surveyed the Glades in years prior and suggested that Fairfax purchase the property. The Glades were so named because of the swampy area along Deckers Creek where trees grew.

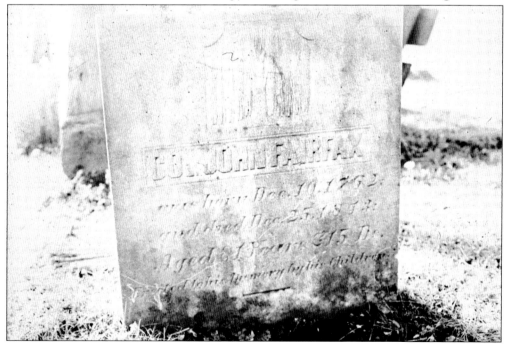

Fairfax soon became a prominent area resident, operating a gristmill and serving as justice of the peace, sheriff, a member of the county court, and a colonel in the Virginia Militia. By the time of his death in 1844, he owned 2,000 acres. This photograph of his tombstone was taken in 1933. (Courtesy WVRHC.)

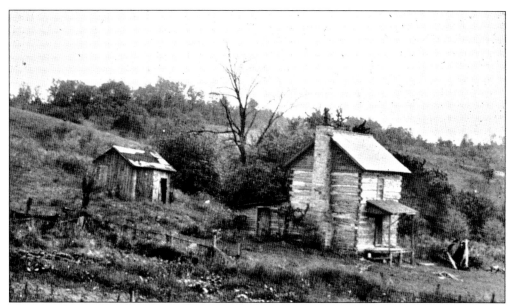

After purchasing the Glades, Fairfax built several slave cabins on the property. He built this cabin, which was still standing in 1933, for his slave foreman, Watt, who "worked faithfully for the Fairfax family for many years." Watt is buried in the Fairfax Cemetery, located on the hilltop behind the cabin, along with Colonel Fairfax and his family. (Courtesy WVRHC.)

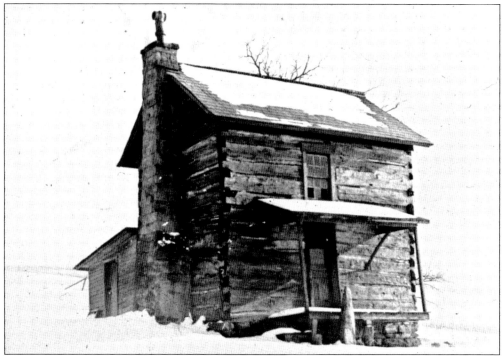

In 1935, the Arthurdale fourth-grade class recorded the history of the cabin as follows: Arthurdale "was all woods, except there was just a little cleared space where the cabin was. The cabin was a big one for those days. It was two stories high and had two rooms downstairs . . . divided by a dog-run." (Courtesy SCRC.)

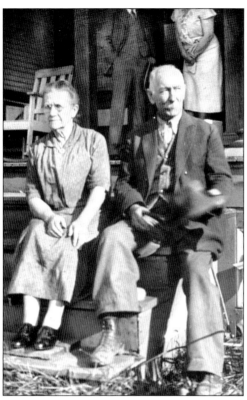

Originally from Pittsburgh, Richard Arthur operated hotels, owned an electric company, and worked as an engineer for steel companies before he decided to retire to West Virginia and become a farmer due to the stresses of city life. He purchased the Fairfax property in 1900. (Courtesy WVRHC.)

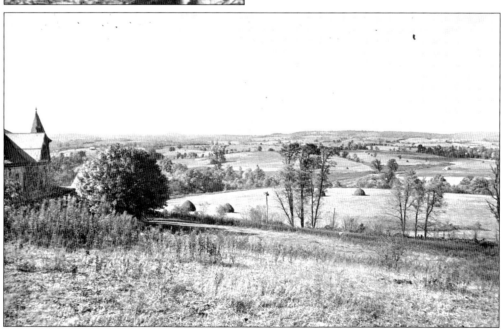

After purchasing 600 acres in 1900, Arthur proceeded to build a stock to include Bourbon-Wilkes horses, pedigreed Jersey cows, Irish white chickens, and Japanese gamecocks, valued at $75 a pair. Arthur grew his farm to 1,200 acres, on which buckwheat, oats, and wheat thrived. (Courtesy Library of Congress; print obtained from WVRHC.)

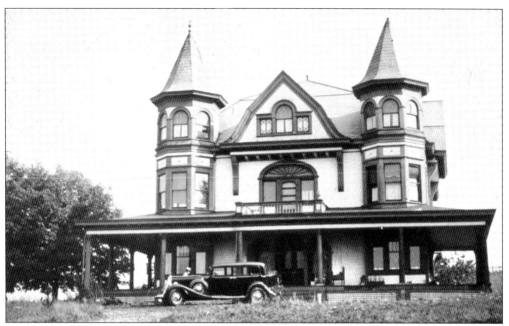

Arthur built this Victorian mansion in 1903, which featured 23 rooms, steam heat, running water, and indoor plumbing. Although he enjoyed initial success as a farmer, Arthur began losing money on his farm and in 1920, started leasing his property to sharecroppers. (Courtesy WVRHC.)

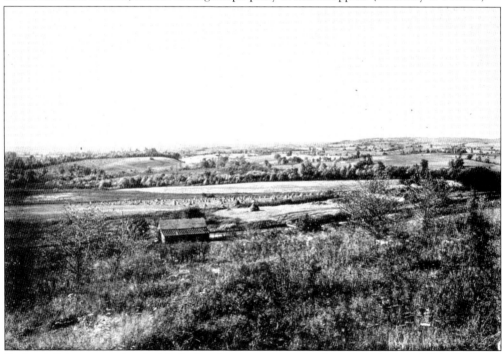

Bushrod Grimes negotiated with Arthur for an option on his farm, seen here in 1933, which was about to be taken by the state for taxes. Louis Howe advised Grimes not to spend more than $25,000 and keep secret the federal government was the buyer. The two parties eventually settled on $35,000 for the property, including the mansion. (Courtesy Library of Congress.)

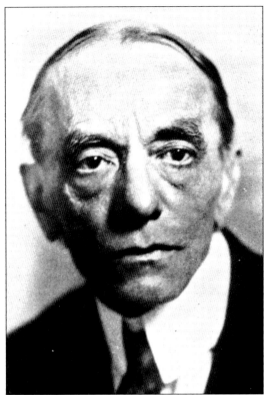

Known as the "man behind Roosevelt," Louis Howe served as a personal secretary to FDR. Howe had great influence over the president and first lady and was often the lone "no" man that challenged the president's policies. Howe routinely cut through red tape to further the Arthurdale project, which he supported until his death in 1936. (Courtesy WVRHC.)

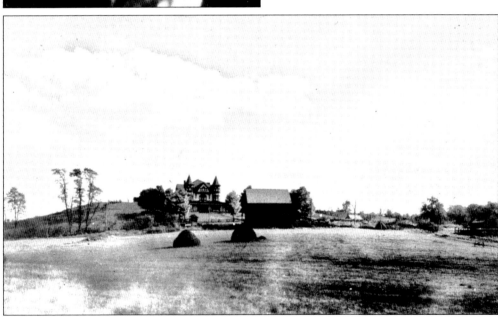

H. B. Allen, a West Virginia University professor took this photograph of the Arthur farm in 1933. An early advocate of the homestead program, Allen sat on the homesteader selection committee with several local and federal government officials, including Alice Davis, Bushrod Grimes, and Eleanor Roosevelt. He photographed his visits to the community, documenting the construction of Arthurdale. (Courtesy WVRHC.)

3.

16. Attitudes: What particular farm jobs do you like best to do? _____

    What particular farm jobs do you most dislike? _____

    Have you ever swapped labor or farm work? _____
    If so, what and how? _____
    What things have you most frequently swapped? _____

    Have you borrowed or loaned farm or garden tools with others? _____
    _____ If so, what? _____
    What is your favorite recreation? _____
    e.g. fishing, hunting, etc.
    What games do you like to play with others? _____

    What sort of work or play do you like best to do to spend your
    idle hours? _____

17. Ambitions: On what sort of a farm would you like to locate? _____

    Would you quit farming if the mines opened up full time? _____
    Where would you like best to settle down if you could be helped?
    _____

    How much education would you like your children to get? _____

    What occupations would you like your boys to take up? _____

Selection of homesteaders began in the fall of 1933, and by mid-October, over 600 applications had been received. In order to narrow the list of applicants, the federal government placed West Virginia University in charge of developing a process to select homesteaders. This is one page of a questionnaire applicants had to complete as part of the homesteader selection process. Applicants had to have a fairly complete knowledge of farming, be physically fit, have a certain level of education, and show "proper attitudes and ambitions." Interviewees were asked about former employment, family history (including mental health), and religious practices. Farm-experience questions included knowledge of gardening, crops, poultry, cows, hogs, and horses. Applicants were even asked to trace their left and right hands for the selection committee to note any defects in form and evidence of manual labor.

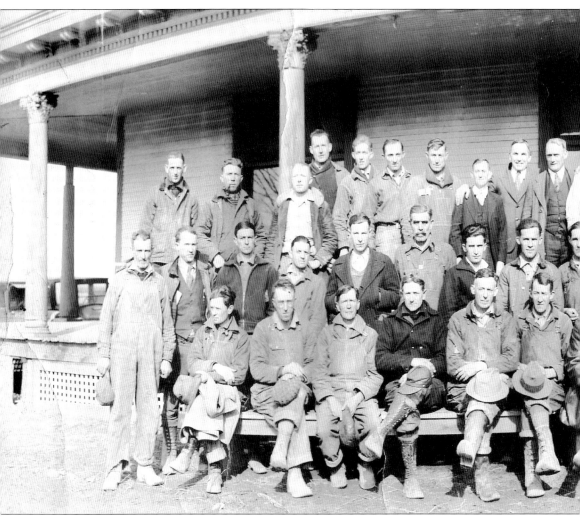

During the winter of 1933, the first 50 Arthurdale homesteaders were selected, some of which are pictured here on the porch of the Arthur Mansion. Most homesteaders were native West Virginians, half were miners, one-fourth were sawmill hands, and one-fourth were farmers. Despite constituting over 80 percent of the population in Scotts Run, foreign-born whites and African Americans were excluded from consideration. The selection committee gave numerous reasons for the segregation, but in reality, the committee felt pressure from locals who held protest

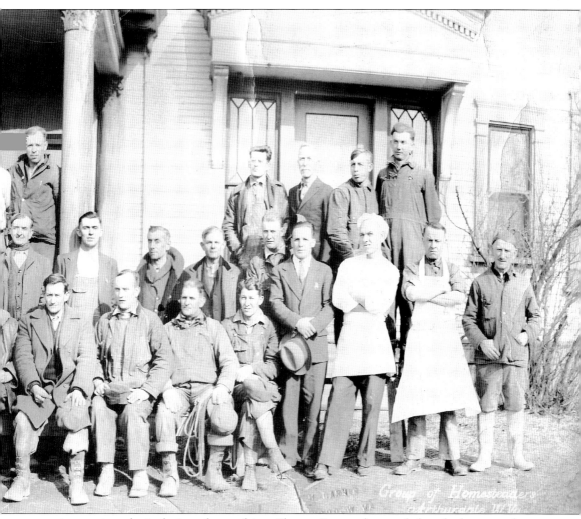

meetings against the inclusion of non-whites. Eleanor Roosevelt appealed to the homesteaders to reconsider, but in a letter to the first lady, the Homesteaders Club upheld the decision to keep the community segregated. Plans were discussed to create a black homestead in Monongalia County, but they were scraped when the Resettlement Administration absorbed the Division of Subsistence Homesteads in 1935.

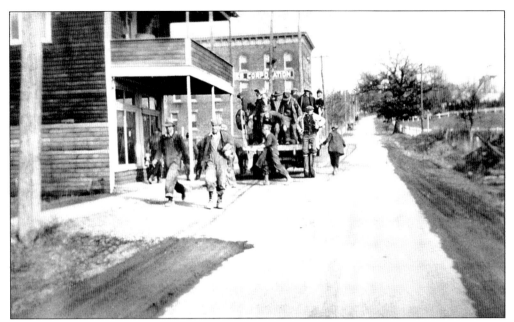

After being selected, 18 to 20 families moved to Preston County, while the rest remained in Monongalia County waiting for their homes to be constructed. A county health officer checked all the homesteaders who came to the work site for physical well-being. Bushrod Grimes persuaded a department store in Morgantown to provide the homesteaders with credit in order for them to purchase work clothing.

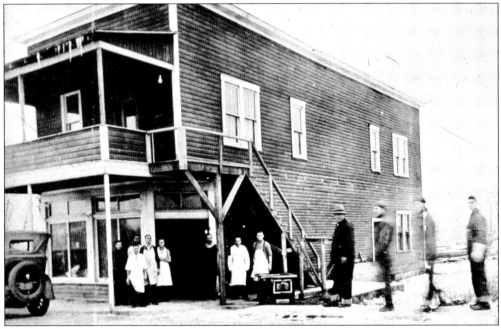

Homesteaders stayed at the Arthur Mansion and the Red Onion, pictured, in Reedsville while constructing their homes. Homesteaders paid $1 a month for lodging and meals. Those who stayed at the Red Onion had to follow rules, including shaving once a week, taking a mid-week bath, and making their own beds. Lights out was at 10:30 p.m. (Courtesy WVRHC.)

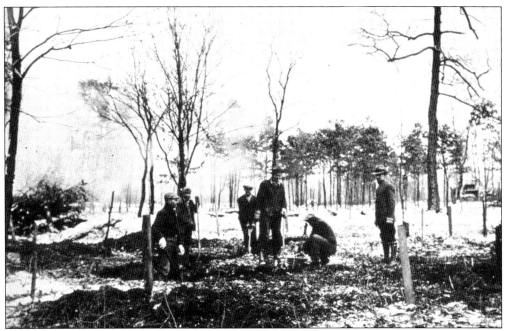

As soon as they were selected, homesteaders began clearing the land. Workers from the nearby Civilian Conservation Corps camp helped homesteaders thin trees. However, due to the drainage issues in the community, plans to grub stumps had to be abandoned, and labor focused on completing plowing for the next year. (Courtesy WVRHC.)

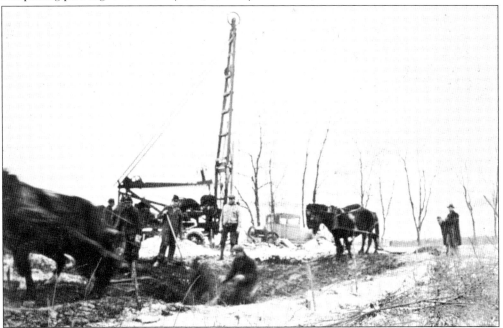

Homesteaders excavated basements, including the first basement in November 1933, pictured. However, excavation had to be put off several days due to the harsh weather conditions. By the end of the second week, excavations were complete and footers poured for only two houses. (Courtesy WVRHC.)

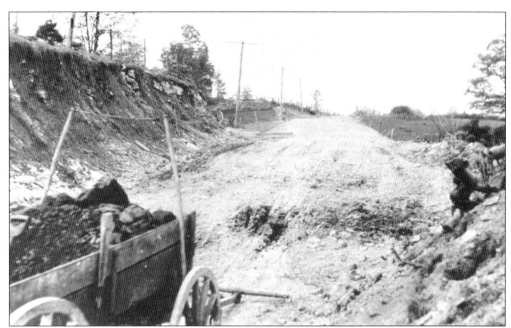

In addition to clearing land, building homes, barns, and fences, workers also constructed over 13 miles of road in Arthurdale. Roads were named after the Washington, D.C., alphabetical system of roads, ranging from A Road to Z Road, and were finished with red dog, the burned by-product of slag piles. Jesse E. Clark took these road-construction photographs. Clark served as project time keeper and road overseer.

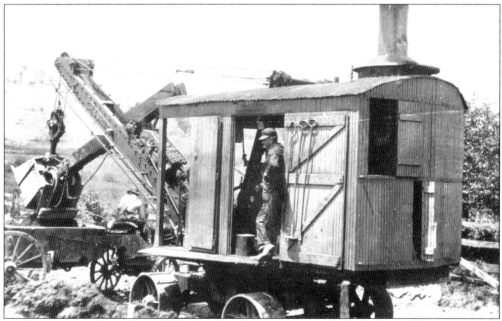

Homesteaders worked 48 hours a week at $3 a day. Despite the long workdays and harsh weather, morale stayed high. One homesteader wrote of his fellow workers, "[w]hen the work of excavating for the basements of their new homes was given to them, they used their picks and shovels with more energy than was ever used by them in loading coal in the mines."

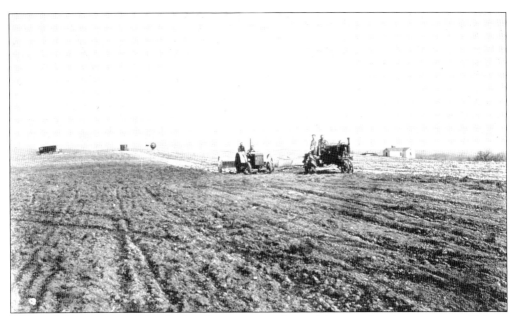

Although large areas of the Arthur Farm were acidic and low in phosphate content, Grimes asserted that it would be particularly fertile once drained and limed. Intense plowing began in the winter of 1933 in order for the ground to be ready for spring crops. Every available plow team in the area was hired at $5 a day. (Courtesy WVRHC.)

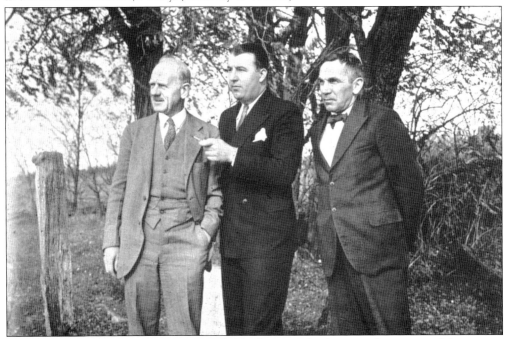

West Virginia congressman Jennings Randolph also proved to be an avid supporter of the project. He said that the community was an "experimental laboratory of the great homestead program. Success here means happiness to thousands of others in homesteads throughout the nation." Randolph is pictured (center) with community planner John Nolan (left) and project manager Bushrod Grimes (right). (Courtesy WVRHC.)

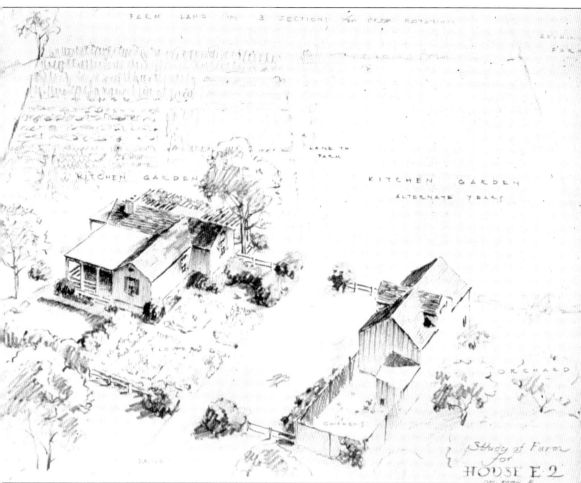

Famed city planner John Nolan devised the first plan for Arthurdale, arranging houses in groups of 20, with the land divided in the form of gardens. President Roosevelt and Bushrod Grimes objected and wanted the homesteads laid out in small, five-acre farms. Architects Walter Trevvett and Benjamin Lane Smith replaced Nolan and soon devised a plan to appease Division of Subsistence director M. L. Wilson, Grimes, and Roosevelt. Grimes suggested that half of the land be farmed intensively and the other half be planted with soil-improving crops for annual rotation, as is indicated on the farm plan above. Land was also set aside for livestock, fruit trees, and vines. In an article for *Atlantic Monthly*, William Brooks proclaimed that on these new farms, the homesteaders could "face to the sky instead of to the earth, to watch the long summer wane, and the color come on the mountains, and the snow fall and pass . . . instead of being shut away among the slag pile down in one of the 'hollows.' " (Courtesy WVRHC.)

Three

A NEW WORLD

From 1933 to 1937, the federal government built 165 homes in Arthurdale. The three different styles of homes all featured electricity, indoor plumbing, and refrigerators. Because these amenities were rare for rural America, critics charged that money was being spent in Arthurdale like "drunken sailors." Added to budget overruns, came additional embarrassments, including foundations that did not fit the homes. Local and national newspapers covered the unfolding events, complaining of oversize budgets and lack of planning.

The initial financial plan called for $2,200 to be spent on the homes, on par for the average cost of homes in 1933. After adding individual sewers and wells, electricity, and refrigerators, the final costs per unit totaled $8,500. Despite the budget overflows, Eleanor Roosevelt reassured the homesteaders that the expenses with the first 50 homes would be assumed by the federal government. The first lady insisted that "no community should be expected to pay . . . [the costs of a social] laboratory for the whole country." A purchase price for the homesteaders was set at $2,500.

In June 1934, Eleanor Roosevelt attended the dedication ceremony for Arthurdale, along with West Virginia congressman Jennings Randolph. The first lady expressed her hope for the project when she addressed the community. "I want you to succeed, not only for yourselves, but for what it will mean to people everywhere, North, South, East, and West, who are starting similar projects. You are the first, and your success will hearten these people."

By 1937, Arthurdale was complete with homes, a center complex, an industrial factory, an inn, a service station, and state-of-the-art schools. The homesteaders were now ready to begin their new lives in their new community.

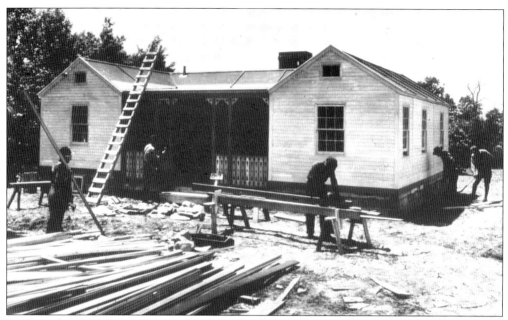

In November 1933, Louis Howe ordered the first 50 houses from the E. F. Hodgson Company of Dover, Massachusetts. The Hodgson Company was one of the first companies in the country to market prefabricated homes. The company's 1920 catalog stated, "thousands of people in every climate of the globe . . . are today living, sleeping, playing, and working in Hodgson Portable Houses." (Courtesy Library of Congress.)

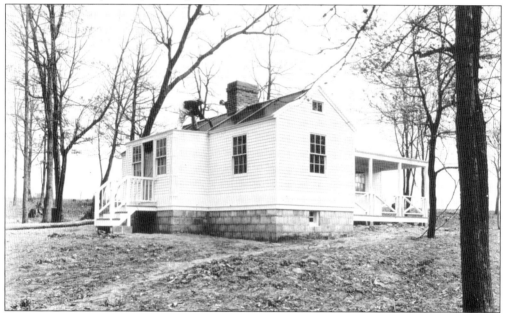

The Hodgson Company proclaimed that its homes "have stood on bleak islands in the most exposed parts" of the New England coast, Maine, and Labrador. However, critics wondered how the $15 wood-burning stove and kitchen range were to heat homes in below-zero temperatures, which were frequent in Preston County. In order to provide additional insulation and more square footage, workers excavated basements for each home. (Courtesy WVRHC.)

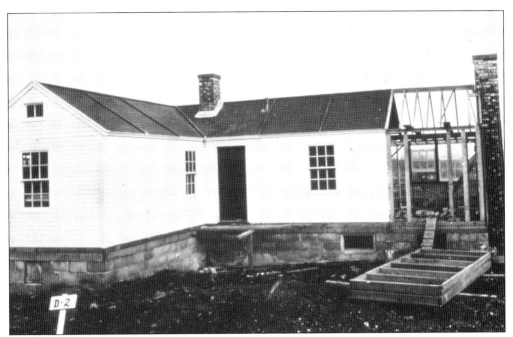

When the Hodgson homes arrived and the prefabricated sections were bolted together, it became apparent that the sections did not fit the foundations already built, and some of them were as far off as 8 feet. Architect Eric Gulger, appointed to correct the construction problems, decided to rebuild and add to the homes in order to reach the foundations. (Courtesy WVRHC.)

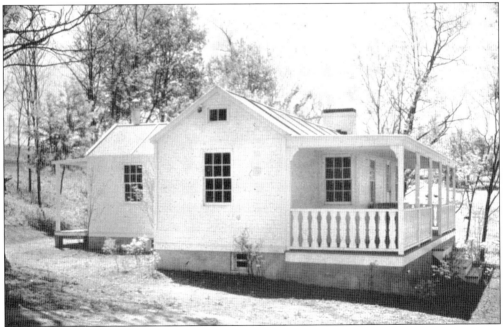

All the homes in Arthurdale had separate wells with electric pumps and individual septic systems. Because of the foundation fiasco, plumbing lines already laid had to be ripped out and new lines installed. In some homes, whole furnace units had to be relocated. However, once constructed, the cottages dotted the picturesque landscape of Arthurdale. (Courtesy WVRHC.)

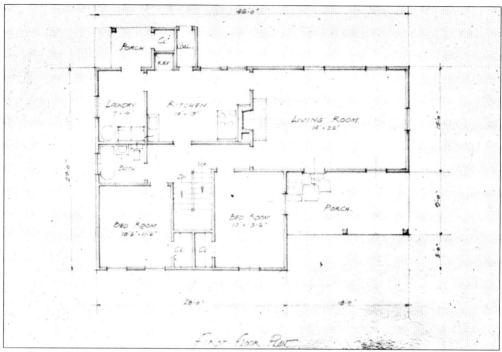
Hundreds of workers, including Civil Works Administration and Federal Emergency Relief men, helped complete nine Hodgson homes within the first 10 days. The homes all differed slightly, featuring four to six rooms in either an I, L, T, or H floor plan and set on two to five acres of land. (Courtesy WVRHC.)

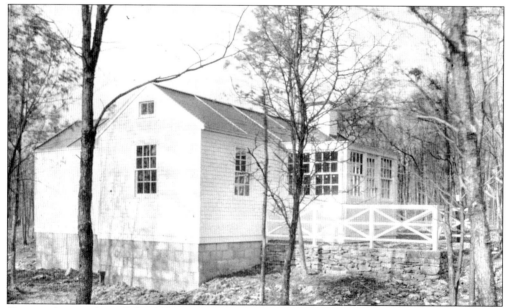
One resident explained the difference in Scotts Run and Arthurdale. "At Arthurdale when you cleaned, it stayed clean. We had a new house with no bangs or scars—and it was heated. It wasn't like the other place where the railroad track was up above the house and every time the train came by the dust would sift down on you." (Courtesy WVRHC.)

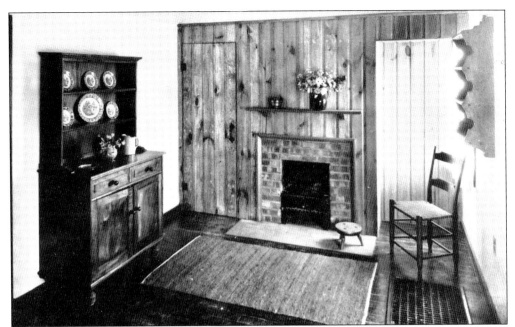

Eleanor Roosevelt, along with her close friend and business partner Nancy Cook, developed interior design plans for the homes. Funds from the Civil Works Administration paid women to make curtains, sheets, and pillow cases for the houses. In addition, each home was supplied with blankets, quilts, bedspreads, towels, and rag rugs. The Mountaineer Craftsmen's Cooperative Association provided the handcrafted furniture, including one double bed, four single beds, two chests of drawers, three tables, and if needed, a crib. Additional furniture could be purchased by the homesteaders through a deduction in their pay for work on the project. (Courtesy Library of Congress.)

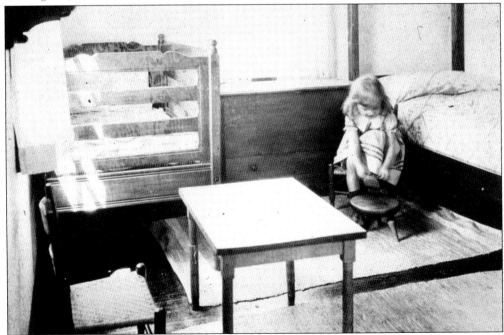

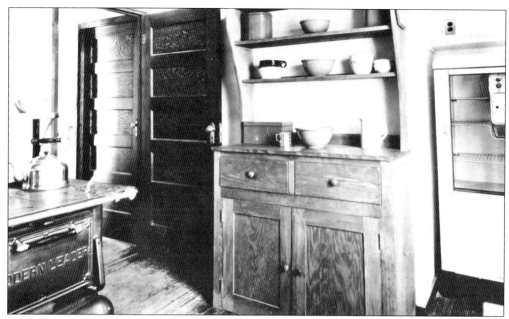

After a visit to see the completed homes, Eleanor Roosevelt noticed that the refrigerators, for which she had personally shopped, had not been included. She immediately began to find out why the refrigerators were not in the homes. After a conversation with the first lady on the subject, Louis Howe issued a threat "to fire the man in charge of electric matters." (Courtesy Library of Congress.)

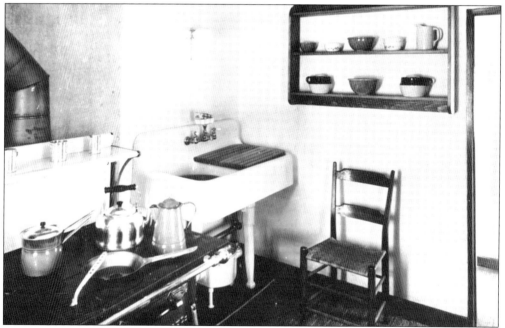

In addition to refrigerators, running water was also a new luxury for the homesteaders. "You have no idea what that meant," said Glenna Williams years later. "We'd never lived in a house with running water. You had rain barrels outside . . . and if it didn't rain for a while you were getting low on water to wash your dishes and to wash clothes." (Courtesy Library of Congress.)

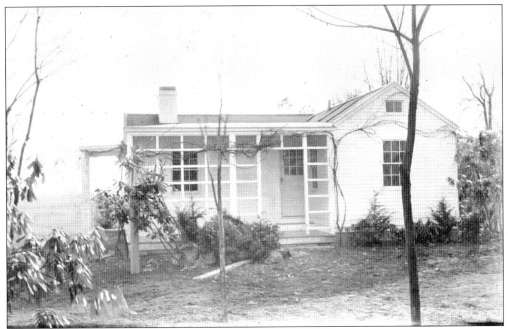

T. D. Gray, a landscape specialist from West Virginia University, completed landscaping plans for the homes. Native plants and shrubs, including rhododendron and bittersweet, were transplanted from nearby woods and set around the homes. Wild grapevines were even woven in trellises on the homes. By July 1934, forty-three of the first 50 homesteads were occupied. (Courtesy WVRHC.)

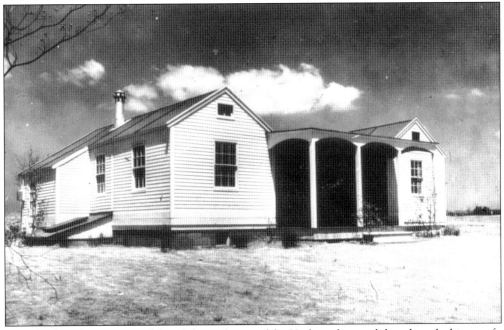

A study after a heavy rain and found that only two of the Hodgson homes did not have leaking roofs. Without downspouts, water ran through the ceiling, under doors, or soaked through walls. Within two years, wells became contaminated in the lower part of Arthurdale, and residents were asked to boil drinking water until a central system was installed. (Courtesy Library of Congress.)

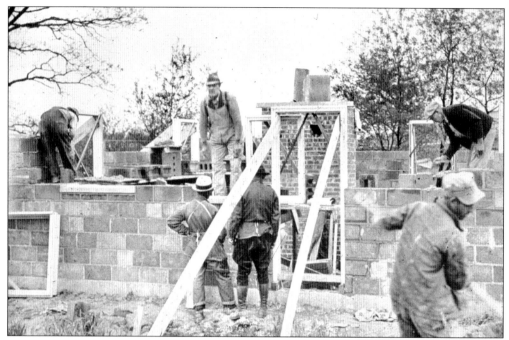

Construction began on the second group of homes in December 1934. Project architect Eric Gugler was charged with designing a suitable home for the community. Gugler soon became involved in designing the White House executive office building and could not complete designs for the homes in Arthurdale. Steward Wagner, a consultant in the Housing Division of the Public Works Administration, was hired to design the 75 homes, on which construction was completed in 1935. Wagner homes had cinder-block foundations, a cinder-block or wood frame on the first floors, and wood-frame siding on the second floors. The Wagner homes also had individual wells and a central sewage-disposal system. (Courtesy WVRHC.)

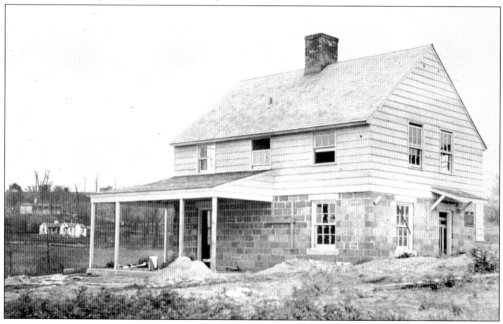

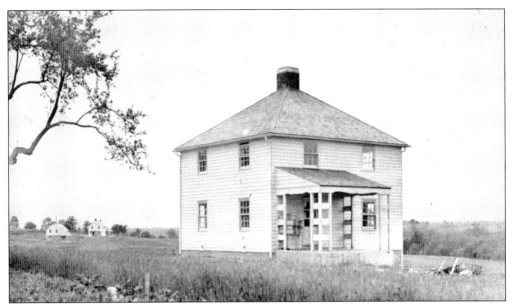

The Wagner homes ranged from five to six rooms. Only six of the Wagner homes had hip roofs and basements, and an example is pictured. The major calamity with the Wagner homes was that their pine and oak parquet hardwood floors bowed in the winter due to being laid directly onto the cement foundations. (Courtesy WVRHC.)

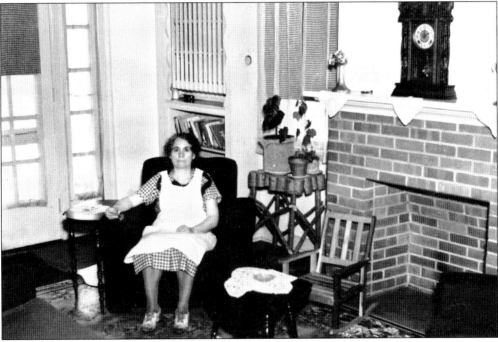

The Wagner homes used coal stoves for cooking and coal-fired furnaces for steam heat, with radiators located in each room of the house. The kitchen featured pantries and birch wood cabinets donned with copper fixtures made by the Mountaineer Craftsmen. The homes also had large closets, built-in bookshelves, and a laundry tub located in a room with a window. (Courtesy Library of Congress.)

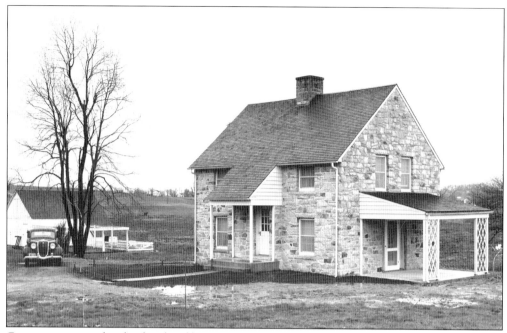

Construction on the third style of homes began in the summer of 1936 and finished in 1937. Stonemasons began quarrying the 2,000 stone blocks for the homes a year prior to construction. The stone homes had two basic styles: one-and-a-half-story bungalows and an English Tudor style, pictured. (Courtesy Library of Congress.)

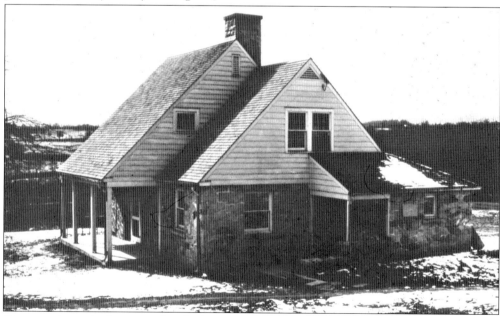

One new issue the homesteaders had to grapple with was paying electric bills. The federal government went into negotiations with the Preston County Light and Power Company, whose rates for Arthurdale almost doubled those for other local residents. By 1937, the administration had settled a sliding-scale rate from four to two cents per kilowatt for usage. (Courtesy Library of Congress.)

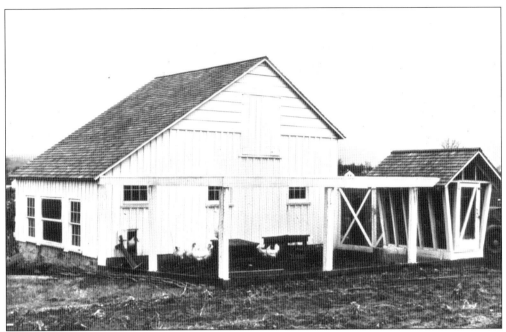

By 1937, all 165 homes for Arthurdale had been built, and all the homesteaders had moved into the new community. All but seven homes included barns, as well as hog and hen houses, pictured. One hundred and eight of the Wagner and Stone Homes also had root cellars. WVU's Agricultural Department showed the homesteaders the best methods of planting and cultivating crops. Homesteaders supplied meat, fruits, and vegetables for their families and most of the time had additional produce to sell. Although the first year was difficult, 81 homesteaders produced over 5,000 gallons of canned vegetables, 1,000 gallons of fruit, and tons of squash, potatoes, pumpkins, cabbage, and root crops with an estimated value of over $14,000. (Courtesy Library of Congress.)

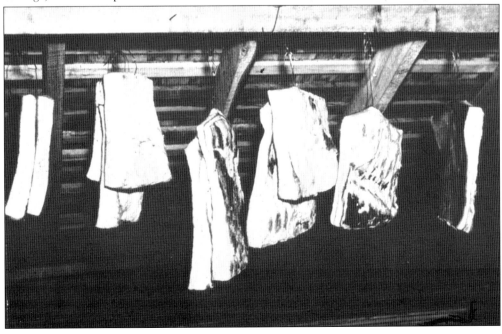

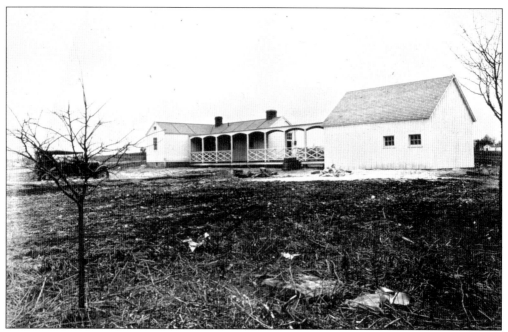

In an article about the community, one writer described Arthurdale as "beautiful on Sundays. Visitors . . . listen with awe to the plans for the school, the church, and the community center. They think it is wonderful the way all the homesteaders are going to have an opportunity to learn handicrafts. . . . The homes are like little corners of Arcady." (Courtesy Library of Congress.)

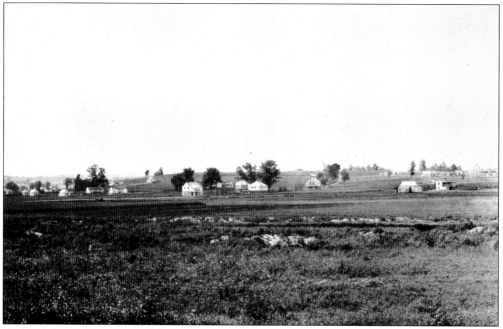

Arthurdale residents enjoyed their new surroundings complete with new homes and farms. One resident described the community as being "like a new world. Outside there was green grass and trees and room to move. You could just stretch your arms out and whistle and not bump into anyone." (Courtesy WVRHC.)

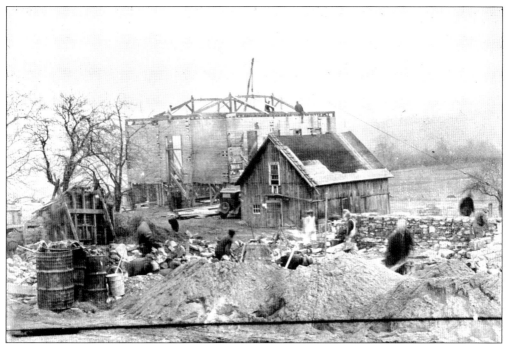

While the first 50 homes were under construction, work began on the center complex in the spring of 1934. The center building of the complex would be composed of an abandoned church and a barn, both purchased by the federal government as an attempt to bring community goodwill to the project. (Courtesy WVRHC.)

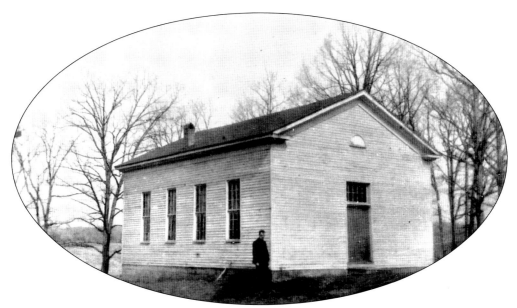

The heart of the Arthurdale community center complex is the Center Hall. Originally a church built in the 1850s, Eleanor Roosevelt saw the abandoned building in a field in between nearby Masontown and Reedsville on her way to visit Arthurdale. It has been stated that the building was used by the community for worship and gathering before soldiers left for the Civil War.

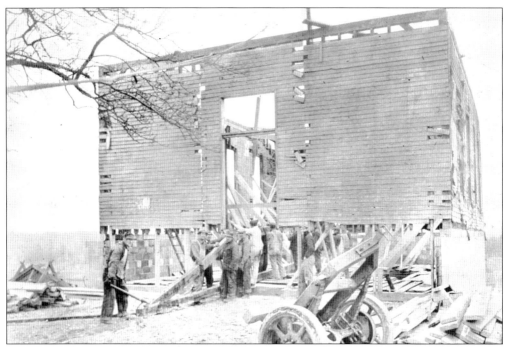
After purchasing the church for $100, workers took the building apart, moved the structure to Arthurdale, and reconstructed it on its present site. The Center Hall served as a meeting space for the community where square dances were held every Saturday night. Workers are shown here moving the church's antique trusses. (Courtesy WVRHC.)

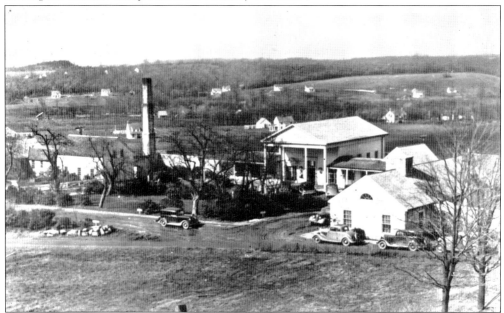
The center was virtually complete by September. Composed of a federal office building, a blacksmith shop, an assembly hall, a general store, a weaving room, a tearoom, a barbershop, and a steam and power plant, the community center was literally the center of community life in Arthurdale. The orchard in front was filled with fruit trees and rhododendron. (Courtesy WVRHC.)

Five
LEARNING BY LIVING

When the first 50 homesteaders arrived in Arthurdale, not only were they given new homes, but also a new community to define. Eleanor Roosevelt saw Arthurdale as an experiment through which the homesteaders were to live. The new homesteaders had to learn to farm, preserve food, raise and butcher livestock, find employment, rid themselves of the individualistic tendencies developed in Scotts Run, and begin life anew.

M. L. Wilson believed that Arthurdale could not be "superimposed from national headquarters"; he wanted the community to be lead by the homesteaders. Despite Wilson's best interests, Arthurdale soon got caught up in red tape, forcing homesteaders to contact federal authorities for minute tasks such as the removal of trees or building fences. Not allowed to fully control their destinies, the Arthurdale homesteaders turned to volunteering and community activities to shape their community—a new community in which everyone was involved.

Founded in 1933, the Arthurdale Homesteaders Club, also known as the Men's Club, was made up mostly of the men who lived together in the Arthur Mansion. The club began working in the school garden, serving on a fire committee, and organizing leisure activities such as a baseball team. The Men's Club also hosted one of the most popular pastimes in Arthurdale, square dancing. Held every Saturday night, the dances featured a professional orchestra until volunteers could be found to take over the duties. A women's club, a singing group, an adult drama club, as well as gardening, crafts, and various athletic clubs were also formed.

Elsie Clapp observed that although the homesteaders were initially very individualistic, they soon "dared to relax and to trust other people and believe in their good fortune." The homesteaders found that they had similar ambitions and began to work toward those shared goals through community work, recreation, and education.

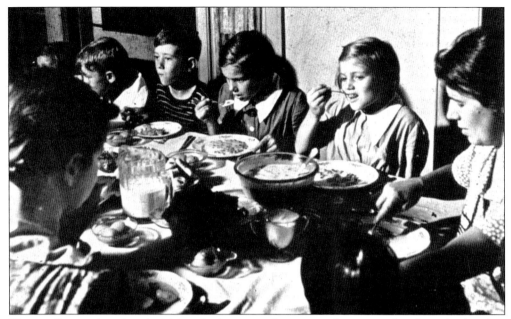

Eleanor Roosevelt enjoyed visiting the homesteads to meet the unique families who lived in Arthurdale. Her visit with the DeGolyer family was documented in the national magazine *Woman's Day*. Clarence worked in the furniture factory and made most of the furniture in their home, including the table seen here, which seated his entire 13-member family. The first lady found the home "in immaculate order and smelling of freshly baked bread." (Courtesy Franklin D. Roosevelt Library.)

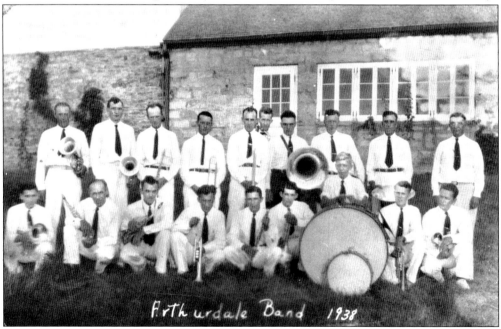

In addition to beginning new lives on their homesteads, the residents of Arthurdale also participated in various community activities. Sponsored by the Arthurdale Community Band, the community organized its first Labor Day celebration in 1938, at which they heard speeches, ate hoe-cooked food, and enjoyed ball games. (Courtesy WVRHC.)

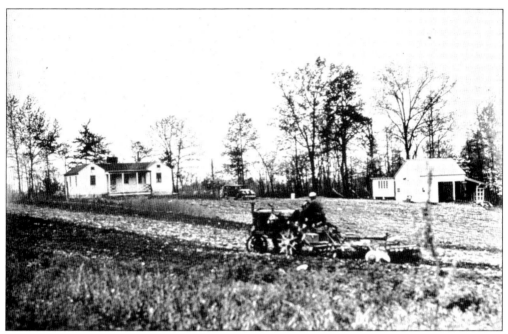

George Beecher, a teacher at the high school, wrote of the homesteaders' initiative to prepare a school garden. "The cost of operating the tractors is being borne by the homesteaders, and much of the work is being done by them after regular hours of work. For the last two weeks, the tractors have been running until dark during fair weather." (Courtesy WVRHC.)

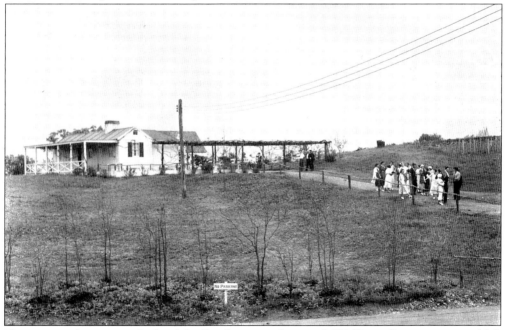

Visitors were frequent in Arthurdale. One homesteader stated, "Hell! . . . Got so a man couldn't set down to his sow belly and turnip greens without some stranger peeking in at the window or walking in to ask fool questions." The homesteaders' drama group wrote a play titled *The Newspaper Spy*, a comic satire that addressed this reoccurring dilemma. (Courtesy WVRHC.)

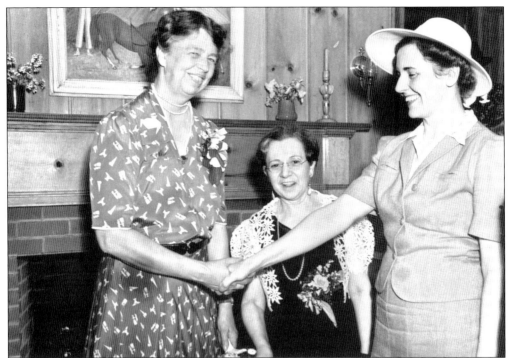

The Eleanor Roosevelt Farm Women's Association, also known as the Women's Club, was formed in October 1934. Although initially only a social club, the association soon formed committees to help families during illness, distribute clean sheets, and organize lectures by doctors. The Women's Club also participated in the hot-lunch program at the school, the weaving room, crafts, gardening, and recreational programs. (Courtesy WVRHC.)

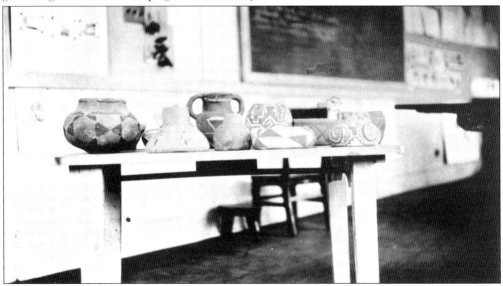

The Women's Club also started pottery classes for 30 men and women. Residents made the potter's wheel and the kiln used at the pottery. The club also held an arts-and-crafts fair, at which all the handcrafted goods created by Arthurdale residents were displayed. The pottery closed during World War II due to shortages of materials and man power. (Courtesy WVRHC.)

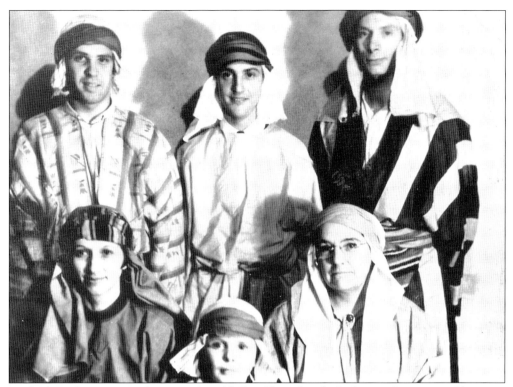

At the first Christmas, one homesteader told Elsie Clapp that she had spent the previous Christmas "living in a house hadn't got no windows—just a door and big cracks in the walls that snow come through something terrible." Eleanor Roosevelt donated money, and a committee purchased toys for the children. The group also decorated a hemlock tree, and students put on a Christmas pageant at the Center Hall.

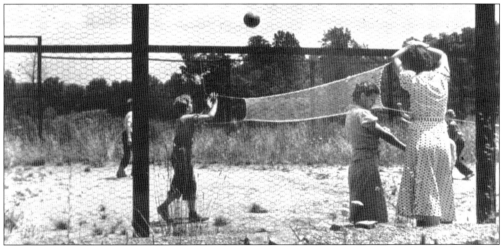

Elsie Clapp also made recreation a focus for all ages because of her "realization that the people needed to learn to play . . . not merely watch others play." The first year of school, basketball, volleyball, baseball, and various other sports teams were developed for adults and children, women and men alike. Square dancing also proved to be a fun, recreational activity for the homesteaders. (Courtesy Franklin D. Roosevelt Library.)

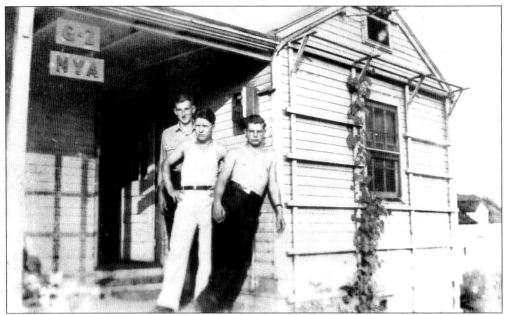

A division of the Works Progress Administration, the National Youth Administration (NYA) provided part-time jobs for youths between the ages of 16 and 25. The NYA differed from the Civilian Conservation Corps because it offered training for various skills, including drafting, Morse code, and radio construction. In the 1930s, Arthurdale NYA projects were mainly manual labor, including improving the community grounds and helping with agriculture.

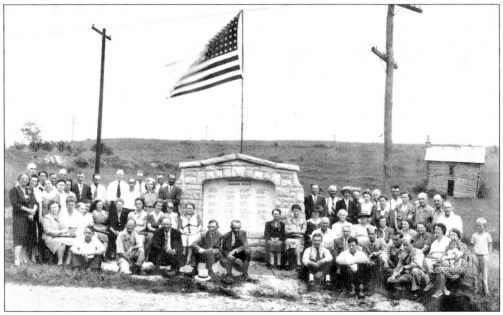

During World War II, the homesteaders in Arthurdale established a committee to collect funds and build a monument to honor the community's residents who were serving the country. The monument is located at the center complex and features the same native stone used on the homes and buildings of Arthurdale. Homesteaders are pictured at the dedication ceremony of the Honor Roll with the Fairfax cabin in the background.

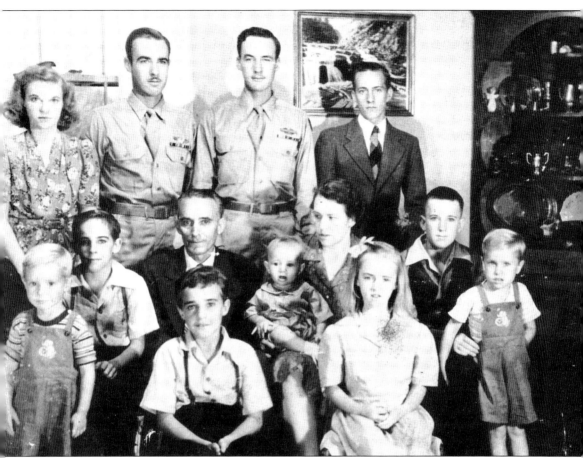

The first lady enjoyed visiting Arthurdale each year to see how the homesteaders were progressing with the creation of their new community and to praise their successes. As well as being a cheerleader for the community, she also took great concern for the welfare of the families. During World War II, when she visited Arthurdale for a high-school graduation, Eleanor Roosevelt heard that Lee Davis, son of homesteaders Frank and Annabel Davis, was missing in action. The first lady immediately set out to find the whereabouts of the soldier, and within three days of returning to Washington, D.C., sent a telegram informing the Davis family that Lee was a prisoner of war. The first lady continually sent Red Cross care package items to be forwarded to Lee, who afterwards said the packages helped him immensely. The Davis family is pictured in 1945. From left to right are (first row) Tim, Tom, Mary Ann, and Rick; (second row) Harry, Frank Sr., John, Annabel, and Bill; (third row) Alice, Lee, Paul, and Frank Jr. (Courtesy Thomas and Loretta Davis.)

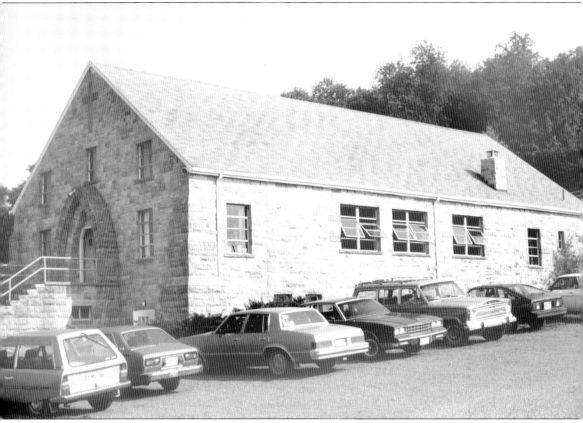

When the homesteaders first moved to Arthurdale, interdenominational services were held at a homestead, then at the Center Hall, and finally in the lunchroom at the new school buildings. After World War II, the community launched a church-building campaign. In 1957, hundreds of volunteers began digging foundations, hauling stone, and driving nails to build a new church. The Arthurdale Presbyterian Church was completed in 1960, and Eleanor Roosevelt spoke at its dedication ceremony. "Arthurdale was begun in hard times," she said, "and the people still have hard times to a great extent. But with the cooperation and great spirit I saw tonight, I am confident that this project has been and will continue to be a great success." The church dedication ceremony marked her last visit to Arthurdale. The former first lady died in 1962. The church is pictured here in 1984.

Five

A Cooperative Community

In 1935, when Rex Tugwell, director of the Resettlement Administration, inherited the project in Arthurdale, he was faced with the looming issue of finding employment for the homesteaders. Tugwell began supporting a cooperative system of enterprise not only because of the lack of industrial development, but also due in part to the comptroller general's refusal to allow Resettlement Administration funds to be used to subsidize private enterprises in Arthurdale. By granting loans to homesteader-operated cooperatives, Tugwell could funnel funds to the project for economic development.

As early as July 1934, the homesteaders expressed an interest in establishing cooperative enterprises. Bushrod Grimes suggested that the men form a branch of the Mountaineer Craftsmen's Cooperative Association operating in Scotts Run. On January 2, homesteaders elected officers and an executive committee for the Arthurdale Association, which was chartered as a non-share corporation on October 22, 1935.

The Arthurdale Association of the Mountaineer Craftsmen's Cooperative eventually took out loans for several cooperative ventures, including a store, farm, inn, industrial factory, and service station, as well as dairy and poultry operations. All business ventures lost money for the association. In his dissertation, *Arthurdale: An Experiment in Community Planning, 1933–1947*, Steven Haid stated in the simplest terms the Arthurdale cooperatives "were poorly conceived, poorly managed, and . . . poorly operated." Low profits and high overhead costs resulted in the cooperatives operating in the red almost from their inceptions.

Although financially unsuccessful, the cooperatives were successful at providing employment to homesteaders at a time when they needed it. The craft cooperatives also provided the homesteaders with skills they could use even after the craft industry stopped operations. The artisans created in Arthurdale continued to practice their craft for the rest of their lives, carrying on the handicraft tradition of the community years after the craft cooperatives closed.

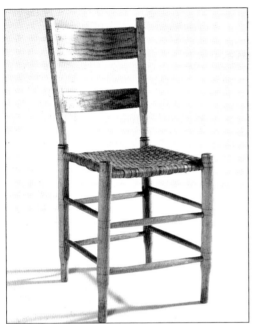 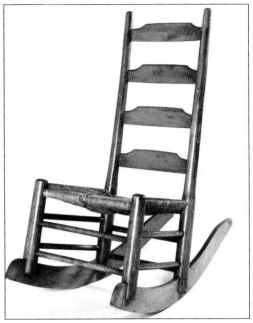

When the American Friends Service Committee came to Scotts Run in 1931, it began a craft program at Crown Mine, hoping to make miners less dependent on coal mining. Bill Simpkin taught miners carpentry and furniture making, while his wife, Ruth, taught their wives weaving and other handicrafts. Samuel Godlove taught chair making. Made of all native wood, Godlove chairs were crafted according to a 200-year-old family design. Kiln-dried rungs and slats joined to green uprights made separable joints, so when the uprights dried, they tightened on the rungs and slats. Weavers crafted the splint-bottom or woven fiber seats for the chairs, which sold for $5. The Crown Mine cooperative eventually formed the Mountaineer Craftmen's Cooperative Association. Items were sold nationwide, and within three years, the MCCA had sold $43,000 worth of furniture. (Above courtesy Jeanne Rymer.)

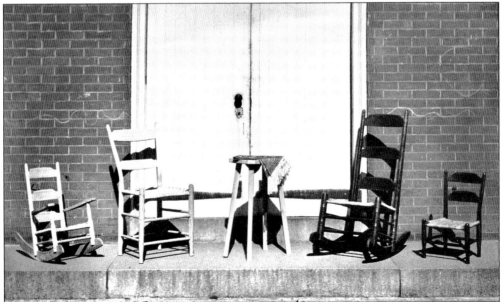

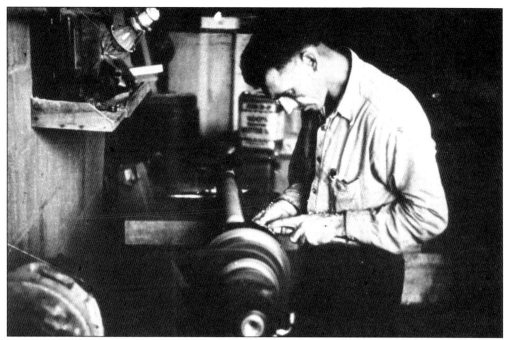

In 1925, along with friend Nancy Cook, Eleanor Roosevelt opened a furniture factory at Val-Kill, on the Roosevelt's Hyde Park estate. Cook found that using machines to cut the furniture, then hand polishing the wood made the furniture look and feel antique. The Arthurdale Association of the MCCA adopted the same method of furniture production. (Courtesy Library of Congress.)

Described as Colonial, MCCA furniture was made of solid, native wood. Items produced included tables, beds, corner cupboards, chests of drawers, stools, and shelves. For these basic items, prices ranged from $4.50 to $75. The furniture operations were initially located in the basement of the Center Hall until workers feared that the operations would burn down the entire complex. A new factory was eventually constructed in 1938. (Courtesy Jeanne Rymer.)

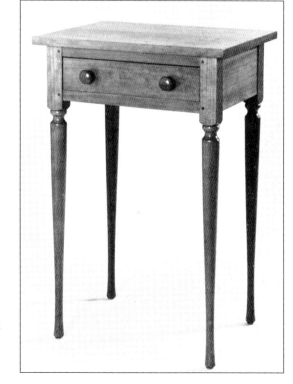

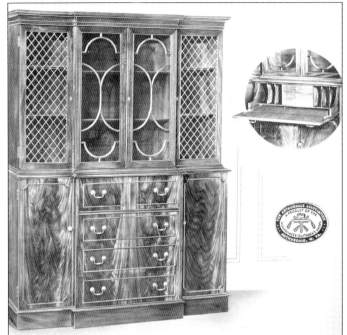

The 500 series of Arthurdale furniture was the first major line produced by the MCCA and was manufactured through 1939. The breakfront cabinets, pictured in an association catalog, were made of solid Honduras mahogany. Base doors and drawer fronts were made of five-ply swirl mahogany face. A writing compartment was also featured in the interior.

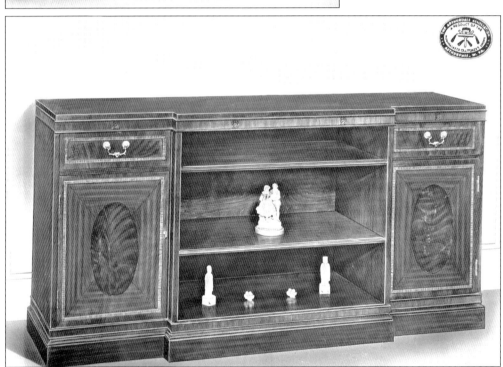

This credenza featured top, ends, and shelves of five-ply striped mahogany. Drawers were faced with swirl mahogany with a border of striped African mahogany finished in a contrasting color. Doors were faced with figured striped mahogany with a boarder of the same wood in natural color and an oval center of crotch mahogany. Base and moldings were solid mahogany with four carved mahogany rosettes in the upper molding. The credenzas also featured heavy brass hardware.

Available in solid rock maple or black cherry, the 700 series, pictured, was a 13-piece set finished with a hand-rubbed lacquer. The series featured mitered and doweled frames, with mortise and tenon construction. Drawer interiors were of dovetail oak, with framed-in bottoms, center drawer guides, and full dust proofing throughout. Items produced included beds, chests, desks, mirrors, and tables of native wood. New styles were eventually implemented in order to broaden the appeal and increase sales of MCCA furniture. On December 9, 1939, the MCCA announced a new line of bedroom furniture, the 750 and 800 series. The 750 and 800 series were simplified in design, resulting in a price reduction.

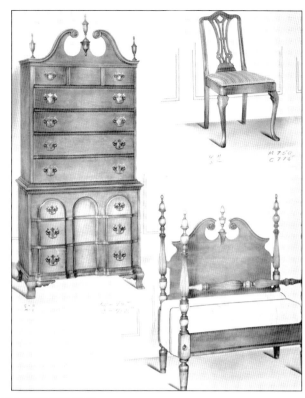

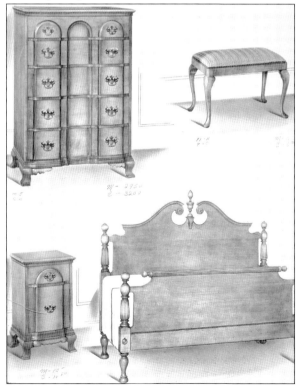

63

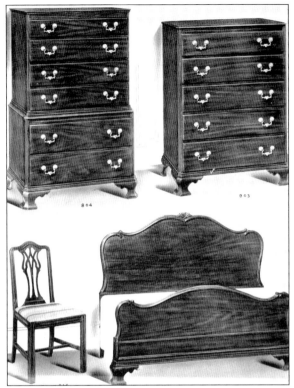

The 750 series was similar to the 700 line except for the elimination of several decorative elements, including blocked fronts, fluting in the post and the foot board turning from the poster bed, and the molding on the headboard and footboard. Shaped partition rails between drawers and lipped drawer fronts were added. The same nightstand could be used for 700 or 750 series. The size of the 800 series, pictured, was the same as the 700 and 750. Although the drawer fronts were the same as 750, the 800 had square-edge tops. The MCCA had originally planned to substitute wooden knobs for brass pulls, but brass pulls are present in the catalog for the 800 series. The 800 series also featured straight fronts on dressing tables unlike the curved ones on the 700 and 750 series.

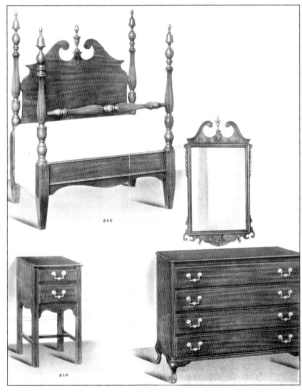

In 1938, the furniture factory moved to a new building, and production increased to fill the orders to furnish the Arthurdale Inn. Despite the increase in employment, work hours, and the introduction of the 900 series of furniture, pictured, the factory continued to operate at a loss through 1940 because of high labor costs. Production costs totaled $1.00 out of every $1.29 in sales.

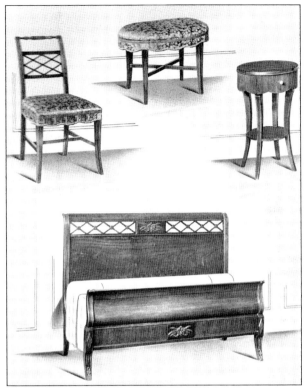

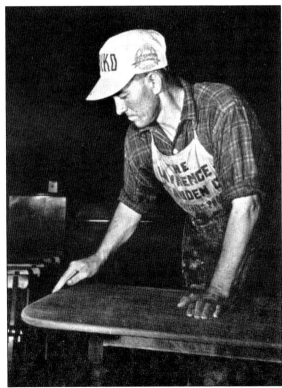

In 1941, the Brunswick Radio and Television Company began leasing the furniture factory. Clarence Pickett stated it was hard to "see men [like Clarence DeGolyer, pictured] who found great joy in producing beautiful handmade furniture abandon it for routine jobs that pay better." Although World War II provided much-needed employment, it marked the end of the craft industry in Arthurdale. (Courtesy Franklin D. Roosevelt Library.)

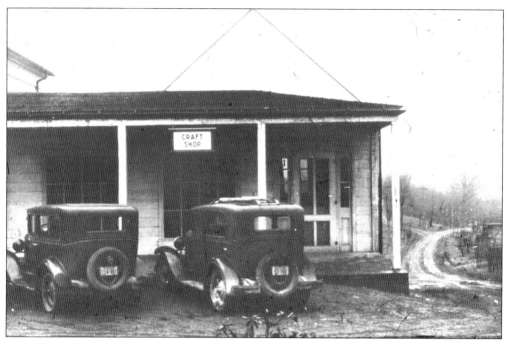

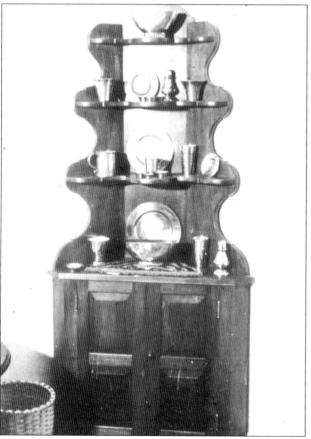

Located in the center building of the center complex of Arthurdale, the Arthurdale Association of the Mountaineer Craftman's Cooperative sold their wares through the Craft Shop. The Craft Shop's building was originally a barn the federal government purchased in order to stimulate goodwill toward the project. The building was included in the design of the Center Hall building, and the roofline on the right side of the building indicates where the barn stands. Patrons to the Craft Shop could visit the showroom and purchase the furniture, copper, pewter, and woven goods on display or make special orders. (Courtesy Library of Congress.)

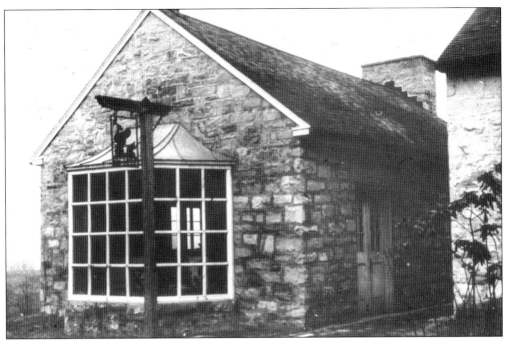

The Arthurdale Association also featured a metalworking shop, which was located in the Forge, a stone building at the center complex. The blacksmiths not only furnished fixtures, locks, and hardware to newly constructed homes, but also created copper and pewter ware that was sold through the Craft Shop. (Courtesy Library of Congress.)

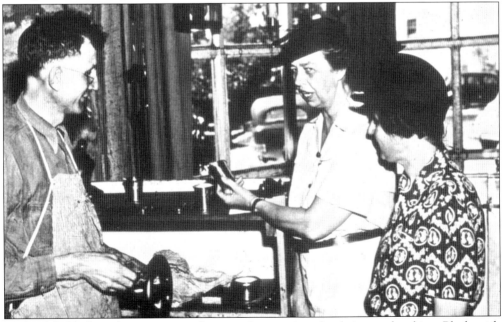

Arthurdale blacksmiths soon received national reputations for their metalworking. Blacksmith Forest Cress is pictured showing pewter ware to First Lady Eleanor Roosevelt from a display case in the Forge. Metal goods were also displayed in the front bay window of the Forge. (Courtesy Franklin D. Roosevelt Library.)

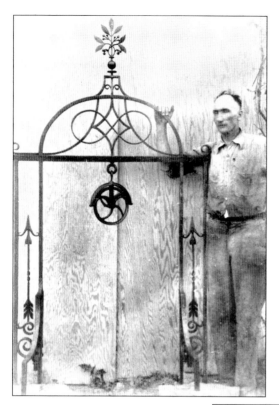

James Londus Fullmer learned to blacksmith when he was 21 or 22. "Lon" remembered "standing under a horse from daylight until the dark of night" while learning his craft. Soon after coming to Arthurdale, Fullmer gained a reputation for his ability to produce replicated antiques. He is pictured with one of the first creations he sold in Arthurdale, a wrought-iron well head.

Fullmer also replicated a Tycho Brahe armillary sphere, which was an astronomy instrument created by 16th-century astronomer, Brahe, who used it around 1575. The sphere was exhibited at the 1938 World's Fair in Seattle and was later transferred to the Smithsonian's Air and Space Museum, where it remains in the museum's collection.

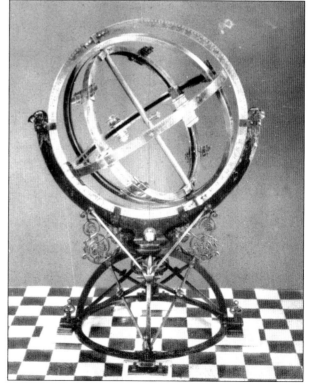

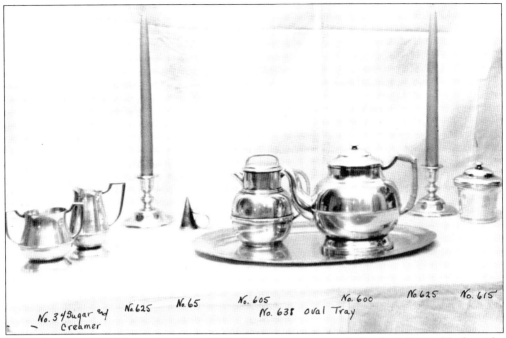

According to a MCCA catalog from 1940, the pewter ware made by the MCCA blacksmiths had a "true antique finish," whose design had been created or copied from actual pieces by the artists. The catalog listed pewter items such as paper knives, candlesticks, bowls, and plates, all ranging in price from 25¢ to $7 for each piece.

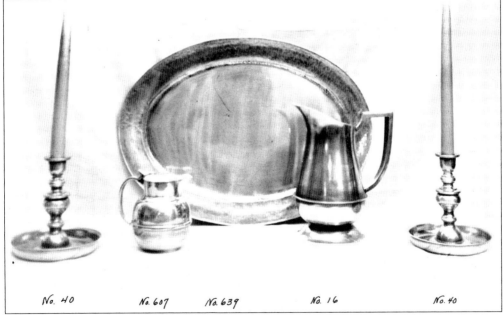

The MCCA catalog billed its pewter work has having the "charm of early American simplicity." The American Federation of Arts even selected the MCCA's pewter candlesticks for display at the 1937 Paris Exhibition to represent American craftsmanship. MCCA artists also created wrought-iron items including wood baskets, fireplace sets, and floor lamps.

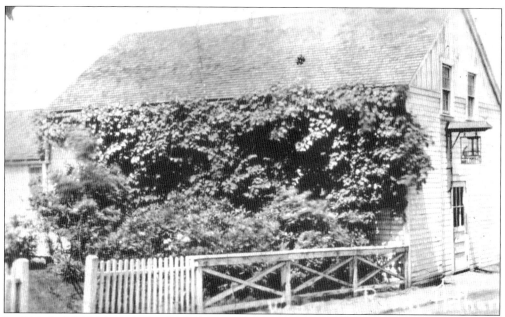

In 1934, the MCCA brought five large harness looms to Arthurdale that had been used at the Crown Mine. Eleanor Roosevelt donated an additional nine looms and brought teachers from Berea College in Kentucky to teach the women to weave. As they became more accomplished, some weavers had skilled homesteaders build more looms on which they could work. (Courtesy WVRHC.)

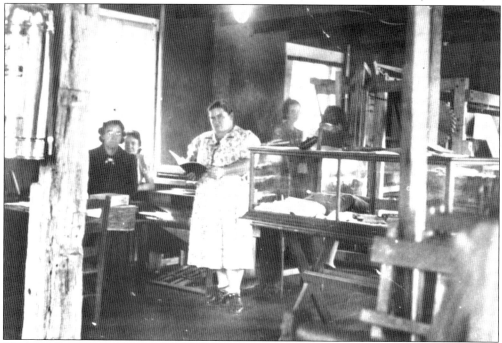

The women wove rag rugs and other items to add to the decor of their homes. Skilled weavers could furnish their entire house with items they had made by hand, including coverlets, aprons, pillow tops, tablecloths, draperies, bedspreads, and clothes. The weavers used linen, cotton, and wool for their material. (Courtesy WVRHC.)

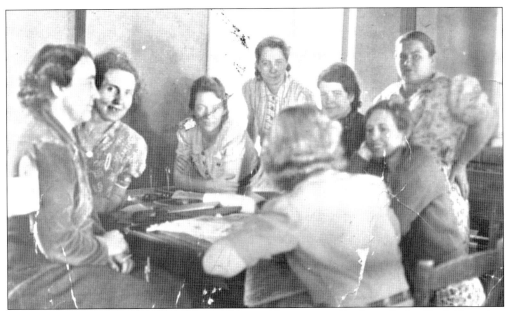

Most of the items created in the weaving room sold commercially through the Craft Shop, but the weavers also filled orders from all over the United States and even from other countries. In addition to making woven goods, they also quilted blankets that were donated to the Arthurdale Health Center and Nursery School. (Courtesy WVRHC.)

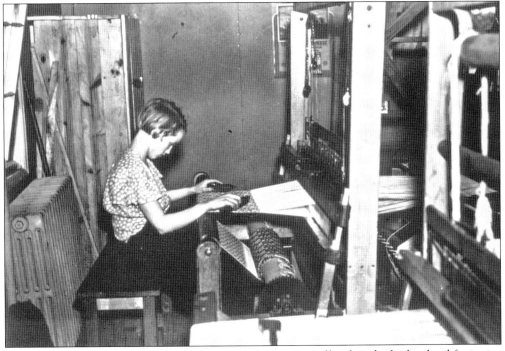

Community interest was so high that a weaving course was offered in the high school for junior and senior girls. In 1939, Eleanor Roosevelt paid for Arthurdale High School graduate Dorothy Mayor to study weaving in Louisville, Kentucky, with master weaver Lou Tate for 18 months. A young girl is pictured working in the weaving room. (Courtesy Library of Congress.)

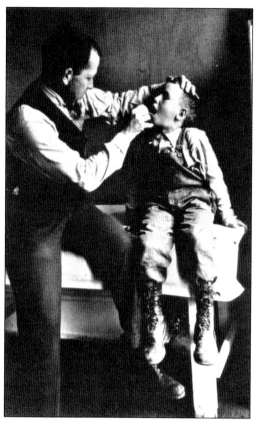

Health problems that had developed prior to moving to Arthurdale plagued homesteaders. During the first year, nurse Kay Plummer provided medical care to the community. Sponsored by the American Friends Service Committee, Dr. Harry Timbres, pictured, became the community's first physician in 1936. Eleanor Roosevelt and financier Bernard Baruch contributed $2,000 to establish a revolving fund for homesteaders who could not afford to receive treatment. The first lady saw the homestead communities as an "unusual opportunity for experiment in socialized medicine and reconditioning of seriously underprivileged groups." After a visit from Dr. R. C. Williams of the Resettlement Administration's Public Health Section, the health program was reorganized into a cooperative system. Homesteaders paid $1 per month for medical care. After the reorganization, the health center operated somewhat in the black until 1938, when membership dropped and an overabundance of delinquent accounts developed. The federal government disbanded the clinic in 1946. (Above courtesy Library of Congress; below courtesy WVRHC.)

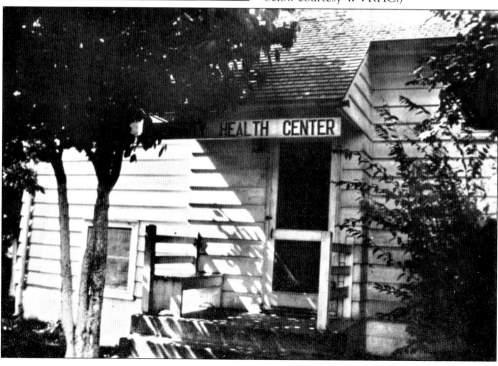

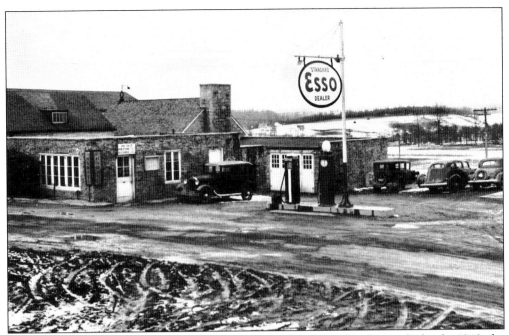

Opened in 1936, the cooperative service station initially operated with a profit, but by 1940, the one-employee operation began showing a loss, and management began complaining of the high cost of gasoline. In June 1941, the service station was leased to the manager, who operated it until the end of World War II. (Courtesy Library of Congress.)

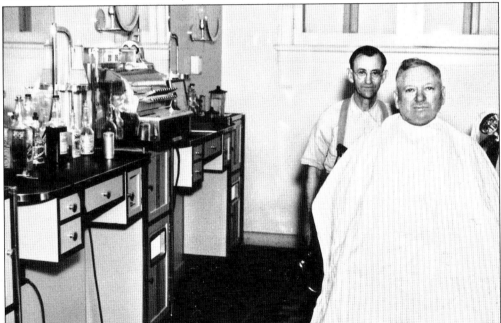

The cooperative barbershop and a tearoom were located in the center building. Two women homesteaders operated the tearoom and sold short orders and confectioneries. The tearoom proved to be economically unsuccessful and closed after only one year of operation. The barbershop was leased privately in 1939. (Courtesy Library of Congress.)

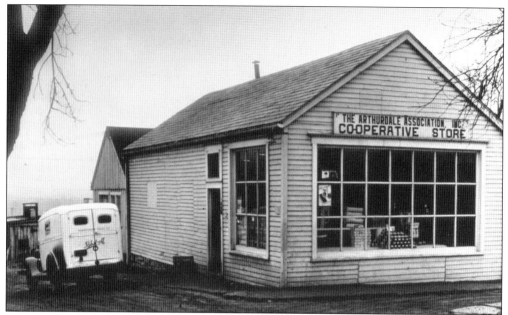

In December 1935, the Arthurdale Association took out a loan for almost $10,000 to establish a general store, which opened for business on January 2, 1936. Sales were to be made on a cash basis, and after one month of operation, the store made a profit of $36.79. It continued to show profits until November 1936. (Courtesy Library of Congress.)

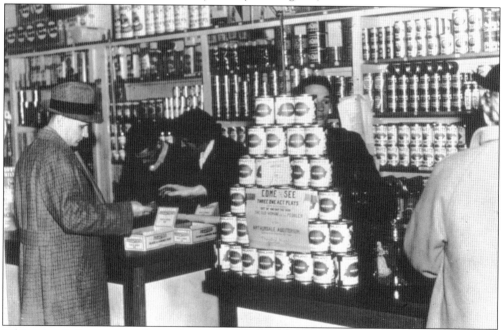

High prices led patrons to shop in Masontown and Reedsville, where prices were lower. Hoping to increase patronage and due to the frequent lateness of payroll checks, the association requested emergency credit not to exceed $10. By June 1937, credit sales doubled cash sales. Most homesteaders met their credit on time with only five percent of accounts delinquent. (Courtesy Library of Congress.)

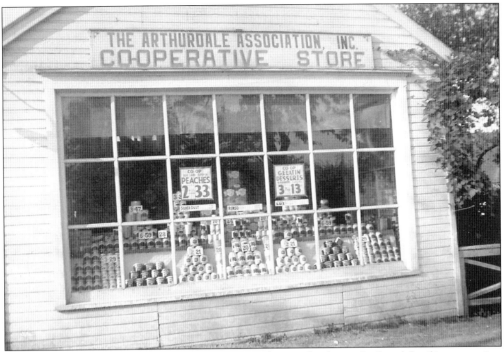

The store eventually expanded to include meat, dry goods, shoes, feed and fertilizer, canning jars, and some clothing in its inventory, but operated at a loss for most of its tenure. Still, the cooperative store produced less of a loss than other cooperative business ventures in Arthurdale until it was leased as a private operation in 1940.

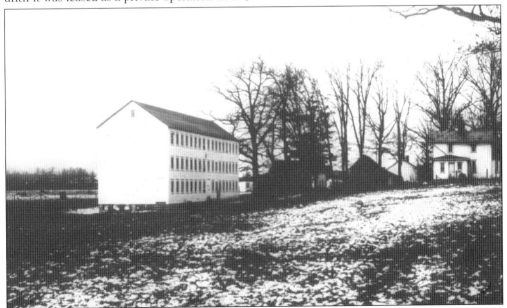

The poultry cooperative began operations in March 1936, and consisted of 2 barns, 40 small houses, and a three-story laying house. Despite raising and selling various breeds of chickens and turkeys, the cooperative operated at a loss, spending too much money on feed and labor. By April 1942, the facilities were abandoned. (Courtesy Library of Congress.)

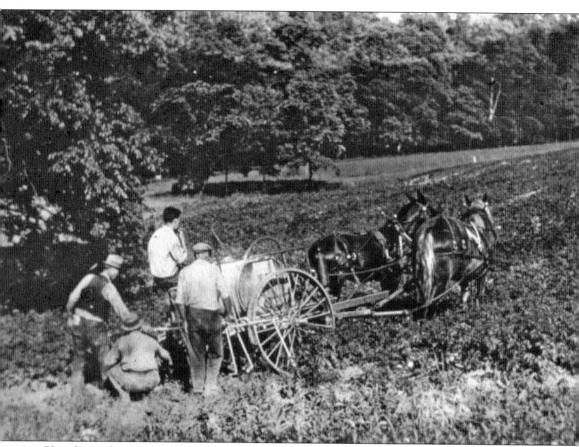

Plans began for a poultry and dairy project in December 1933. The association built a barn in 1937 and in January 1938 purchased a herd of Jerseys. Homesteaders Percy Martin and Clinton Wolfe went to Michigan and brought back the herd in railroad boxcars. The dairy operations began the next month. A 400-acre farm was set aside to produce grain, vegetables, and livestock for use in Arthurdale and for sale to wholesalers. Feed crops were produced, including wheat and oats, but potatoes, which are pictured being sprayed, proved to be the best crop. High labor costs plagued the farm, and after three years in operation, it recorded a $20,000 debt. (Courtesy WVRHC.)

In April 1938, the administration leased the dairy and farm operations to homesteaders Percy Martin and Clinton Wolfe for showing an aptitude for the agricultural work. The two managers made an initial profit, but by 1940, the production once again began operating in the red. The dairy and farm operations were eventually sold to West Virginia University in 1942 for $1. Pictured working on WVU Farm in the early 1950s are, from left to right, Percy Martin, Clinton Wolfe, Frank Smith, and Bill McNelis.

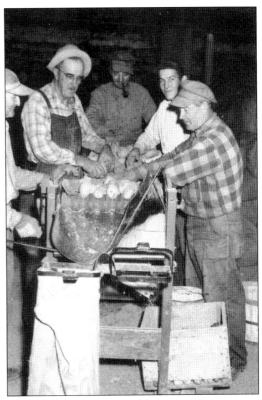

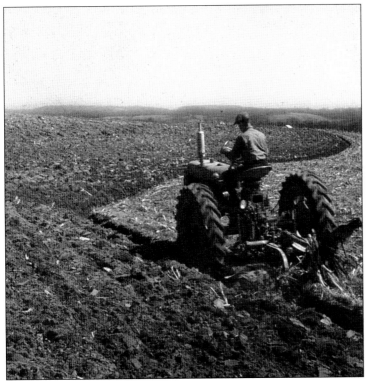

West Virginia University updated the farm and purchased new equipment, such as tractors, hay balers, and combines. WVU also set out to make more of the acreage farmable by laying drain tiles along Deckers Creek—making the land more arable—and by dynamiting open drainage ditches that were clogged with debris. The WVU Reedsville experimental farm is pictured here in 1946.

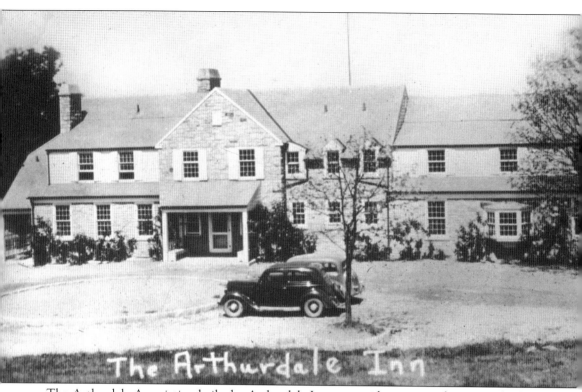

The Arthurdale Inn

The Arthurdale Association built the Arthurdale Inn to provide accommodations to the large number of visitors who came to Arthurdale. When it came time to determine a site for the inn, the Arthur Mansion was foremost on the list. School administrator Elise Clapp argued to save the home, stating it would be a "waste of good material" to tear it down. Despite her arguments, Rex Tugwell ordered the building to be demolished immediately. Stewart Wagner delivered his designs for the $43,000 building, and construction began in December 1936. The inn opened for business in May 1938 and featured 20 guest rooms and baths, a dining room, and a terrace large enough to accommodate 50 people. The MCCA produced all the furniture and fixtures, and the menu included food grown or produced by homesteaders. Like other cooperatives, the inn also produced annual losses. The Farm Security Administration eventually leased out the building to the NYA to be used as a dormitory for their defense-training program in 1942. (Courtesy WVRHC.)

Six

Industrial Development

As early as October 1933, the administration began to pursue employment options for the homesteaders and settled on building a factory to make furniture, equipment, and lockboxes for the Post Office Department. Congressman Louis Ludlow of Indiana wrote to the president in opposition of the project because the Keyless Lock Company, located in his state, "has but one patron and that is the Government of the United States." Ludlow stressed that if a post-office factory would open in Arthurdale and other proposed homesteads, his unemployed constituents would be turned out to "tramp the streets."

During the winter of 1934, issues of monopolies and government competition with private businesses arose in senatorial and congressional discussions and after months of debate, the decision was made to shelve the plans for the post-office factory in Arthurdale. It soon became essential to find a replacement private business that would provide employment to the homesteaders. In July, Louis Howe approached General Electric with the possibility of locating a factory in Arthurdale. A contract was soon drawn, and construction on the factory building began along with selection of homesteaders to work in the factory at 40¢ per hour.

Despite the initial victory in finding a business to locate in the Arthurdale factory, the administration struggled throughout the 1930s to retain a steady source of employment for the homesteaders. In 1940, only 1 homesteader in 166 was working in the Arthurdale factories, not including the craft shops, and the rest were employed by the government or were working off of the project. World War II provided a boost to the economic troubles in Arthurdale. Brunswick Radio and Television began operating in 1941, and other war-related manufacturers provided employment to homesteaders on- and off-site to finally bring wages to an industrial level.

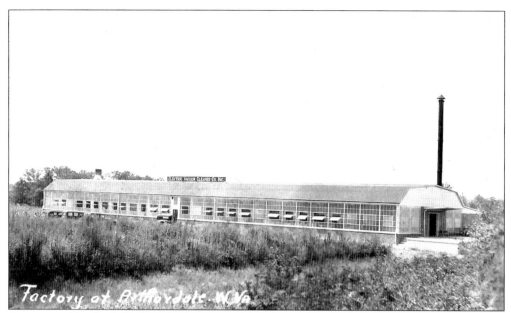

Constructed by the federal government at a cost of $30,664, the Arthurdale factory building was complete in July 1935. The Arthurdale Association purchased the building in January 1936 for $12,804 to house the Electric Vacuum Cleaner Company of Cleveland, a subsidiary of General Electric. Plans included obtaining contracts to supply vacuum cleaners to federal agencies in order to provide employment.

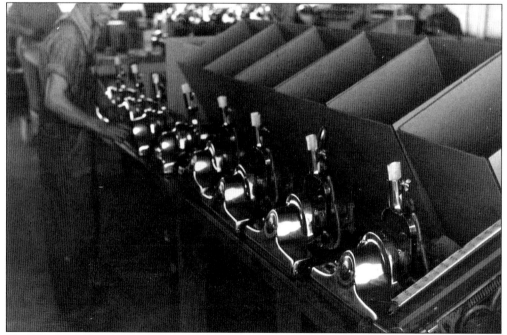

The factory employed 29 homesteaders at its peak because it only had a capacity to produce certain models of vacuum cleaners that were not in great demand. The company began developing a new product line that would necessitate between 50 and 75 employees, but those plans never materialized. (Courtesy Library of Congress.)

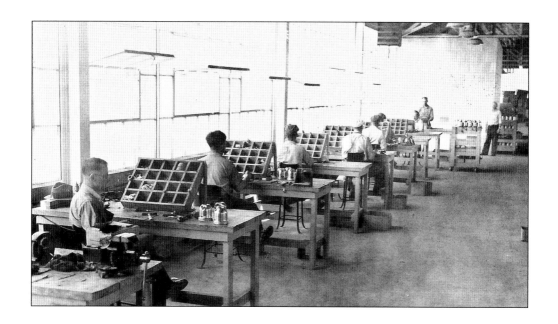

As employment numbers dwindled, the Resettlement Administration began negotiations with the Electric Vacuum Cleaner Company to increase employment. Despite hopes for obtaining more governmental contracts, the factory closed for several weeks in August 1937 for new model changes. By October, it became apparent the factory would not open again when the company cut its workforce in Cleveland by 50 percent. In February 1939, the company cancelled its lease with the Arthurdale Association after operating only 13 months. The Phillip-Jones Shirt Company began operating in the factory in 1937, but because of high wages and low production efficiency, it suspended operations in August 1938. (Courtesy Library of Congress.)

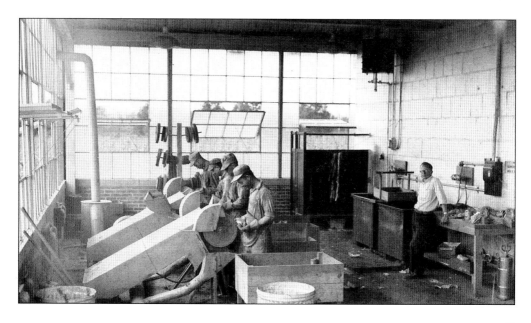

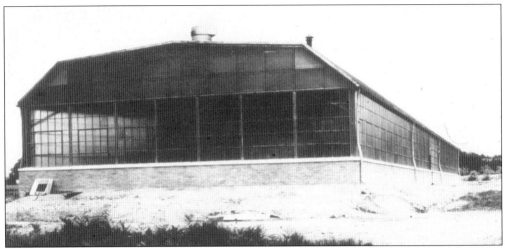

After the shirt and vacuum-cleaner companies ended operations, the Economic Recovery Committee began searching for a replacement business to occupy the factory. From 1934 to 1939, at least 50 different operations were suggested, including manufacturers of pistols, bombs, and even air-conditioned clothing. Most sought public funds in order to make a private profit, and others were just impractical. (Courtesy Library of Congress.)

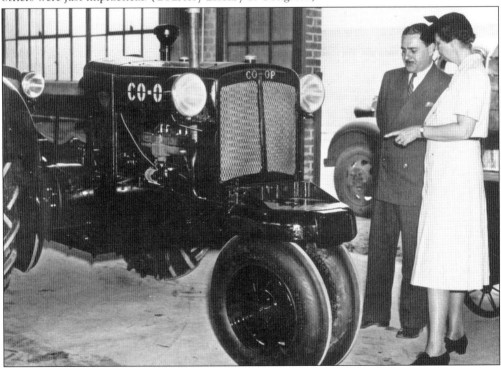

In August 1938, an agreement was reached with American Cooperatives, Inc., to relocate its tractor-assembly plant from Michigan to Arthurdale. The association agreed to provide the building, equipment, machinery, and operating capital for the operations,, while American Cooperatives agreed to lease the building and equipment from the association. Eleanor Roosevelt is shown visiting the tractor factory in 1939. (Courtesy Franklin D. Roosevelt Library, print obtained from WVRHC.)

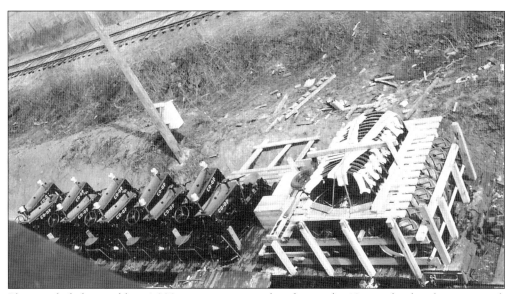

Plans included assembling 1,200 tractors per year, but during the 12 months the plant operated, those numbers were never reached. The association lost money each month the factory operated, and eventually the agreement with American Cooperatives was cancelled in April 1940, after a loss of over $100,000. Cooperative tractors are pictured, along with tires and fenders, ready to be shipped out on the railroad. (Courtesy Jeffrey Zinn.)

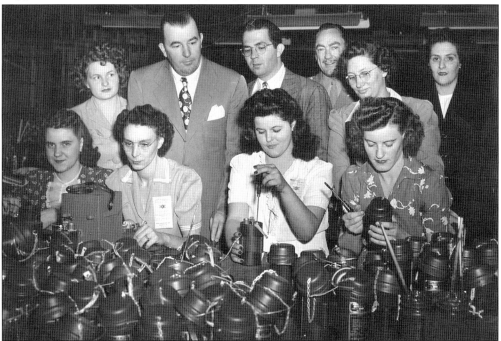

In April 1940, Silman Manufacturing began manufacturing items for the Signal and Marine Corps, including walkie-talkies, flares, and radios. The company employed almost 100 women and operated in two of the Arthurdale School buildings. Assembly-line workers are pictured with Jennings Randolph in celebration of Silman receiving the Army-Navy "E" award for meeting its production quotas during World War II.

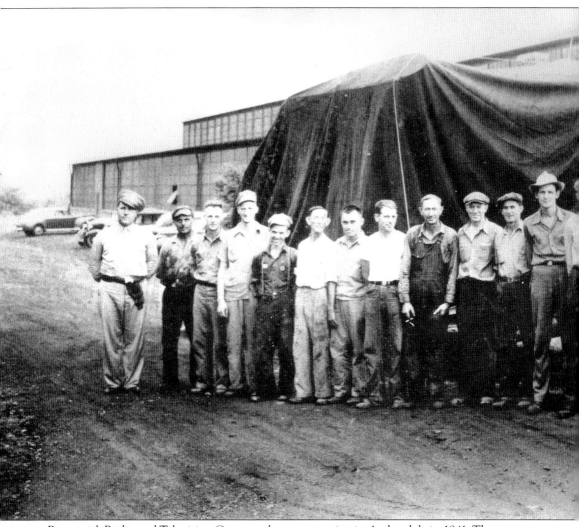

Brunswick Radio and Television Company began operating in Arthurdale in 1941. The company produced cabinets, radio chassis, record players, and speakers. Despite registering wholesale sales in excess of $250,000, by the end of 1942, the company suspended operations. By 1940, war-related production had made its way to Arthurdale and surrounding communities. Homesteaders found work at Silman Manufacturing, back in the mines, and at DuPont in Morgantown. In 1943,

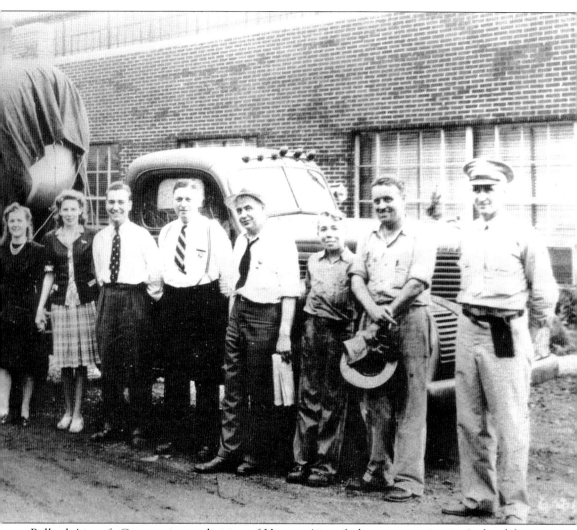

Ballard Aircraft Corporation, a division of Hoover Aircraft, began operating in Arthurdale. The company produced wooden mock planes used for pilot training. It occupied three factories and the inn. Although both Silman and Ballard looked into remaining in Arthurdale, both had ended operations by the end of World War II.

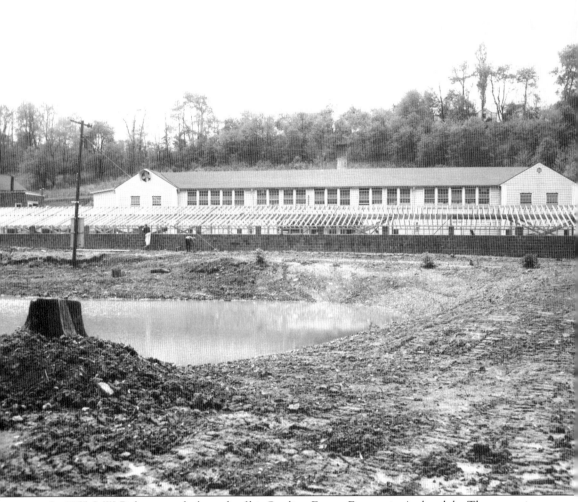

In 1955, J. W. Ruby opened a branch of his Sterling Faucet Factory in Arthurdale. The operations took over the factory building and manufactured faucets and plumbing fixtures. This business operated in Arthurdale until Ruby died in August 1972. Ruby also operated the Sterling Farms in Arthurdale, which was a chicken, turkey, cattle, and horse farm. These agricultural operations were located in the Arthurdale Primary and Nursery School buildings, pictured, in the 1950s. To add to his industrial operations in Arthurdale, Ruby also owned the Arthurdale Inn and purchased an original home. (Courtesy WVRHC.)

Seven

A COMMUNITY SCHOOL

Although Arthurdale suffered from lack of economic development, the community enjoyed many successes, including the creation of a progressive school system headed by Elsie Ripley Clapp. A student of John Dewey, Clapp saw the Arthurdale School as a great opportunity to create a community school "made with the people whose school it is." She had been working in Kentucky at Ballard Memorial School and had found partial success with her community-school program there. Clapp came to Arthurdale as chairman of the Committee on School and Community Relations, and had been asked by Eleanor Roosevelt to visit the community and give suggestions on developing a new school. Soon after her visit, Clapp agreed to become administrator for the new school.

After accepting the position, Clapp began to learn about her new pupils and community. She visited Scotts Run to see the homesteaders' past and realized issues that needed addressing through the Arthurdale school system, including health care, physical education, and adult education. She also picked a suitable location for the school buildings. Clapp told Clarence Pickett that her new school system could not be accomplished unless certain conditions were met, including the necessity of federal support for no less than three years. She also wanted to select her own teachers.

In Arthurdale, the students learned through hands-on activities rather than theoretical learning and undertook projects related to agriculture, construction, and the students' Appalachian heritage. The first lady supported the experimental school system to which she donated money, books, and supplies. As Clapp had hoped, the school had an overwhelming effect on the community. In 1936, Rex Tugwell, head of the Resettlement Administration, reported that "morale at Arthurdale and conditions there were ninety percent better than in any other homestead, entirely due to the school."

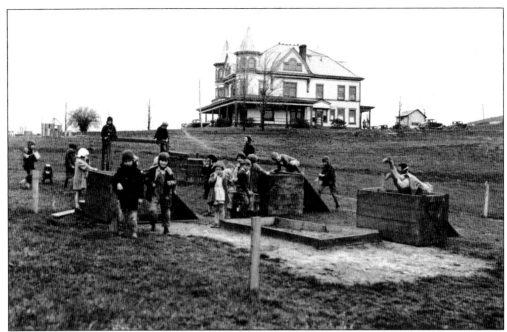
In the fall of 1934, construction on the new school buildings had not started, so Clapp and her teachers worked to get other community buildings ready for use as school rooms. After being used for a year as barracks, the Arthur Mansion was cleared, floors were scrubbed, and walls were painted in order to house the primary and elementary schools. (Courtesy Library of Congress.)

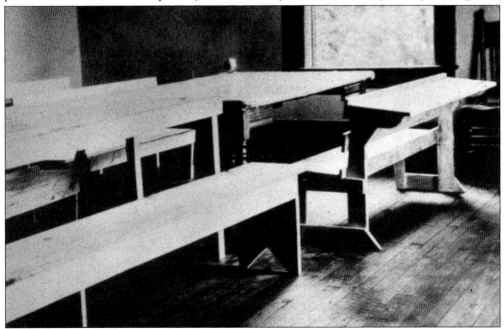
Clapp stated that the homesteaders did not even grumble when it came time to get the buildings ready for school, "indeed they all felt relieved and reassured that there was someone around who believed in having things right for the children." Pictured are the rudimentary desks built by homesteaders for the students. (Courtesy SCRC.)

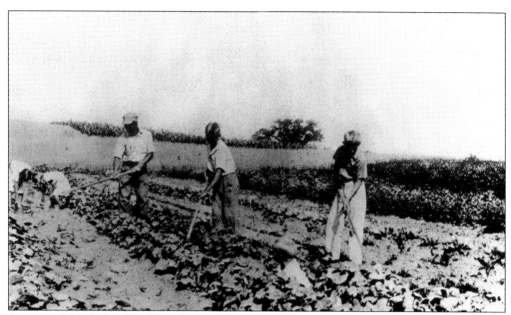

Because of the lack of books and equipment, the community became the students' classroom. When first graders studied farming, they went to a field that was being plowed, saw the threshing of buckwheat and digging of potatoes, and helped milk cows as instructed by the homesteaders. (Courtesy SCRC.)

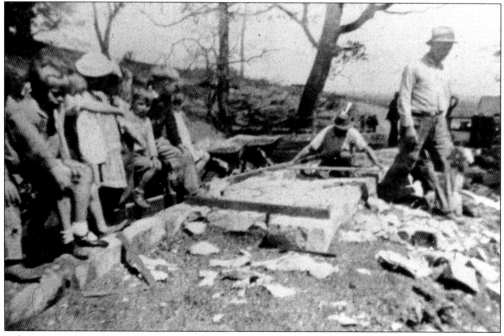

When second graders studied the building of a village, they watched the homesteaders build the homes, dig wells, and lay foundations. Through these projects, Clapp believed the students could identify themselves as homesteaders and take on a greater understanding of their new environment. Here the second-grade class watches workers construct the sidewalk for the new schools. (Courtesy SCRC.)

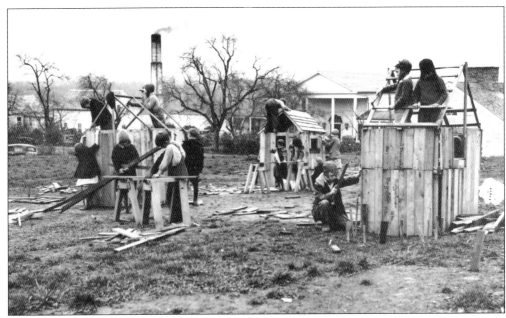

The second grade chose an area that was flat and had shade when it came time to build its own community in 1934. Using scrap materials found in the community, the students developed a village along the rode to the Arthur Mansion. This project helped enhance the children's understanding of fractions, addition, and subtraction. (Courtesy Library of Congress.)

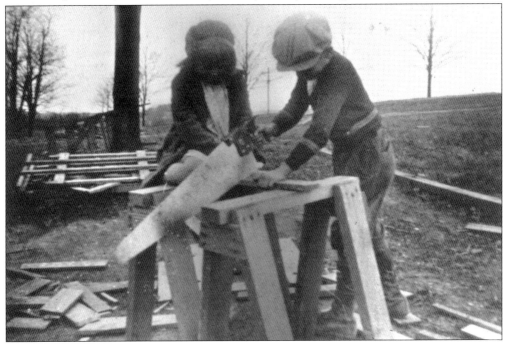

In 1935, the second-grade students included a hospital, a store, two houses, and a farm in their village. The students decided to locate their village near the new nursery school. Because of their studies about farming the year prior, the members of this class took more of an agricultural perspective when planning their community. (Courtesy SCRC.)

In 1934, the Fairfax Cabin was being used for grain storage until the fourth grade used it to study pioneer life. Through the cabin project, the children learned to celebrate their heritage. The fourth grade is on the porch of the cabin behind the third grade, which studied Native American life. (Courtesy Library of Congress.)

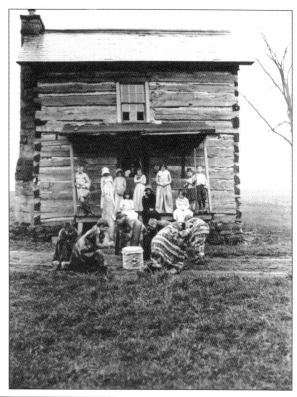

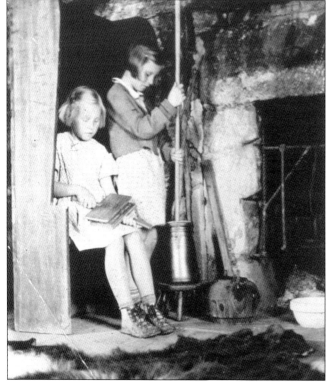

Through hands-on activities, such as carding wool and churning butter, fourth-grade students took on a better understanding of materials. By tanning a hide, they learned what labor and materials went into making a pair of shoes. With the help of the community, the cabin took on the atmosphere of an early pioneer home. (Courtesy WVRHC.)

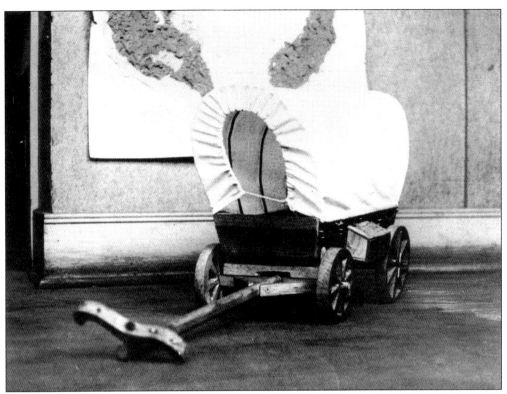

In 1935, a combined fifth and sixth grades studied pioneer transportation and built a covered wagon and a flat-bottom boat. Teacher Inez Funk stated, "[w]e looked for materials and read what we could; what they couldn't read, I would read to them. Then we measured to get our proportions, did the arithmetic and figured that out." (Courtesy WVRHC.)

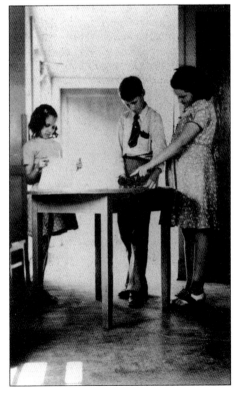

Fletcher Collins wrote that his students "were genuinely surprised at the lack of switchings and knuckle-rappings" given by him. Collins was amazed by the seventh- and eighth-grade students who brought to Arthurdale "stories of blood and thunder" from their previous schools, where corporeal punishment was used to control children. The students created a large-scale map of Arthurdale for their first combined class project. (Courtesy WVRHC.)

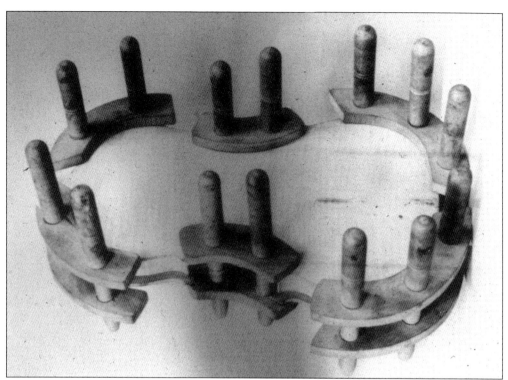

Three boys in the seventh and eight grades became fascinated with the orchestra that played at the Saturday-night square dances. Fletcher Collins, the drama and music teacher, found a local fiddle maker and invited him to Arthurdale in the spring of 1935. The boys produced completed fiddles one year later. (Courtesy SCRC.)

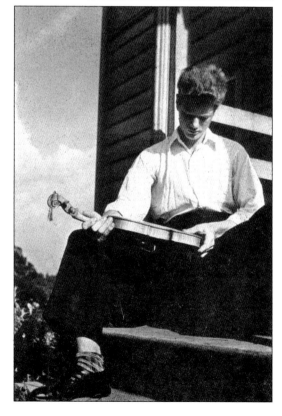

All three boy's fiddles were exhibited at a music festival held in June 1936. Fletcher Collins organized music festivals in Arthurdale in 1935 and 1936 that featured fiddlers, jig-dancing, ballad-singing, mouth-harping, and square-dance contests. Eleanor Roosevelt awarded the winners. Henry DeGolyer is pictured with his completed fiddle. (Courtesy Franklin D. Roosevelt Library.)

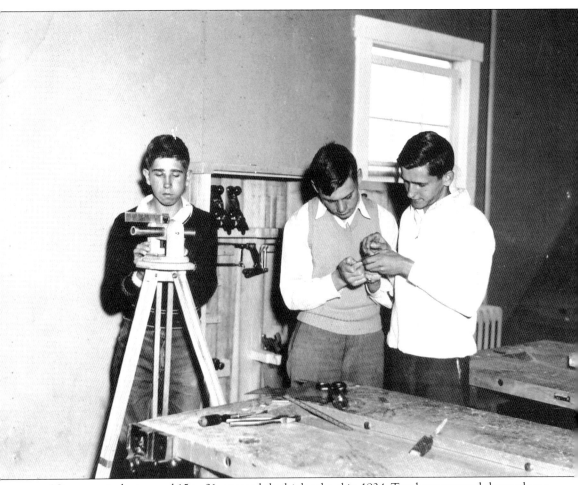

Nineteen students, aged 15 to 21, entered the high school in 1934. Teachers grouped the students based on interests rather than age, and the system worked well. One group studied science and mathematics, along with home economics, shop, reading, and spelling. The second group studied economics, along with history, arithmetic, reading, short hand, and typing. Botany students collected, classified, and mounted specimens found in Arthurdale. Geology students constructed a coal mine. Students undertook practical projects, such as making radios, writing their own ballads, and making surveying equipment. Elsie Clapp also wanted to address education for the number of young people who left school to work in the mines in Scotts Run. She began night classes through which they studied carpentry, electrical work, math, and typing, among other topics. (Courtesy Library of Congress.)

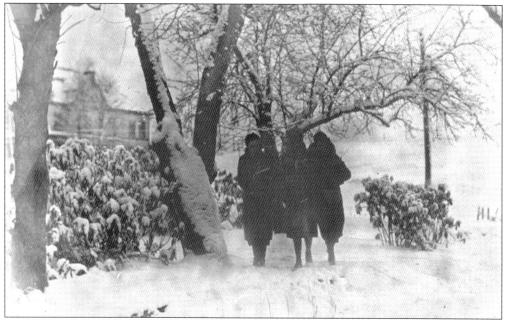

"Learning was made exciting," Annabelle Urbas Mayor reflected on attending school in Arthurdale. "You didn't want to miss a day because if you did someone would know how to do something you didn't know how to do. We learned to weave and plan meals. The first year I took electric shop and we made radios and telegraph sets and sent messages back and forth between buildings. In science class we made a surveyor and in math we surveyed where Route 92 is now. In English class we wrote plays, and made the costumes in home economics." Mayor (right) is pictured with Glenna (center) and June Williams walking to school in 1936. Younger students rode to school on a bus, which is shown below in the winter of 1934–1935 dropping off students at the nursery school. (Above courtesy WVRHC; below courtesy SCRC.)

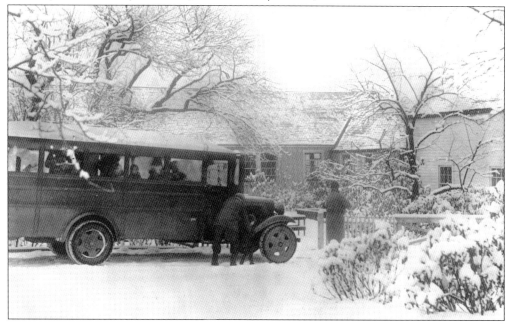

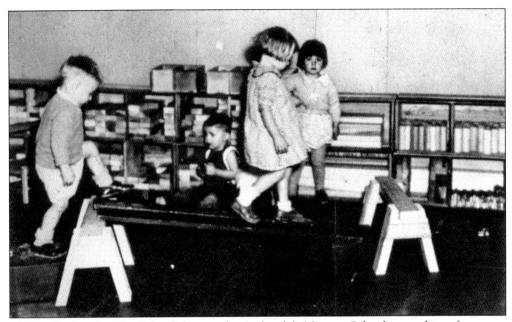

One week after the "Big School" began, the Arthurdale Nursery School opened in a four-room building at the center complex under the direction of Jessie Stanton. Stanton worked previously at the highly acclaimed Harriet Johnson Nursery School. Clapp noted that the nursery school children looked "aged, wizened, wan, and lifeless, they all showed the suffering they had undergone." (Courtesy Library of Congress.)

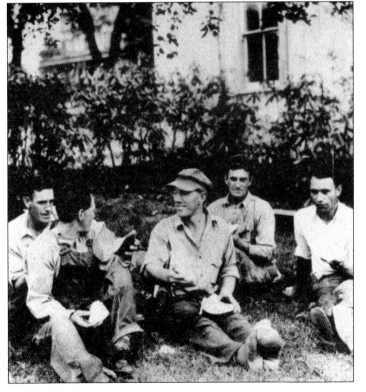

Homesteaders worked diligently to finish the nursery-school building in 10 days. Fathers who worked on the school are pictured taking a lunch break. Despite being over the garage bays where "project trucks roared in and out all day," Clapp believed, the central location of the school allowed mothers to stop by during their days to check on the children. (Courtesy SCRC.)

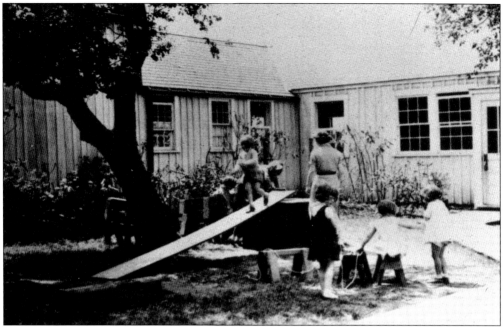

The nursery's playground was consisted of a sandbox, which was made of a shipping crate and long boards used as climbing apparatus. MCCA made sawhorses and blocks. The playground for the four and five year olds was located across the street and also consisted of packing crates, blocks, and sand. (Courtesy SCRC.)

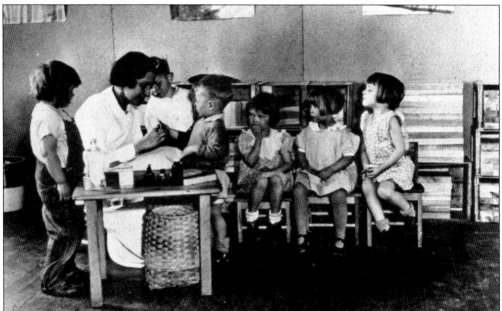

In 1934, Clapp brought in the construction nurse to do daily inspections of the schoolchildren. Her work caught developing colds, sore throats, skin problems, and infectious diseases. Kay Plummer, pictured, took over the next year and continued the work to clear up the children's health problems. By the next spring, skin diseases, such as scabies and impetigo, were eradicated. (Courtesy Library of Congress.)

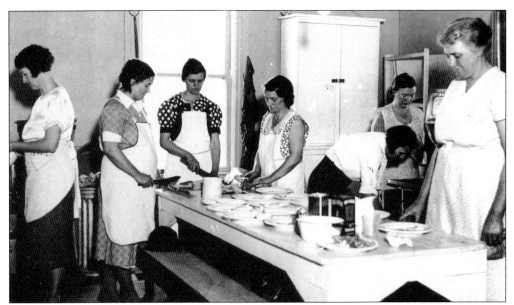

As Elsie Clapp had hoped, the school became the center of activity for the community. Women worked in the kitchen to can the vegetables raised in the community garden. Mothers, through the Women's Club, came by the school each day to cook and wash dishes. The women donated canned goods and vegetables, helping give the students a well-balanced meal. (Courtesy Library of Congress.)

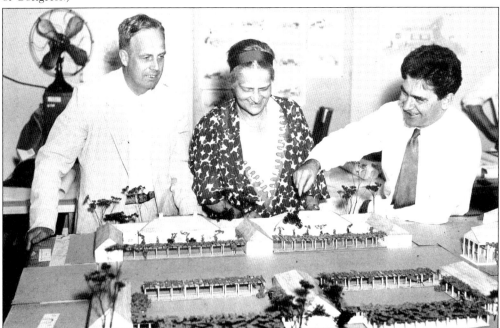

Elsie Clapp is pictured here with Clarence Pickett (left) and Eric Gulger (right), the project's first architect, designing the school campus to be a "village within itself." The complex included playgrounds, gardens, and was comprised of detached buildings to prevent the spread of disease. Plans began on the school in 1934, but due to budget cuts, had to be revised to include only one-third of the original plans. (Courtesy SCRC.)

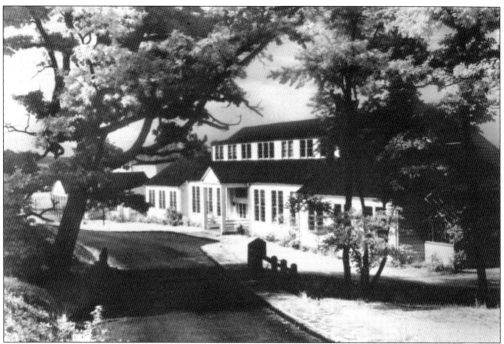

The school moved into six new buildings in the fall of 1935. Planned to house the six upper grades, the high school consisted of eight classrooms, a shop, a science room, and a greenhouse. The upper level housed the library, a pottery room, an art room, and a printing room. (Courtesy WVRHC.)

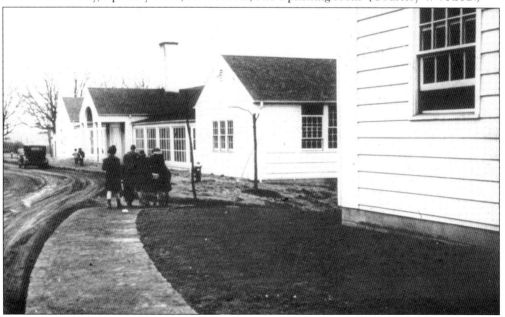

The primary and elementary schools were identical one-story buildings built to accommodate 150 students. The greatest architectural feature on these buildings was the front, which was made entirely of glass. Each room in the buildings had a sink and an alcove workroom. Clapp designed the buildings to be "homelike in character and allow the maximum of sun and air." (Courtesy Library of Congress.)

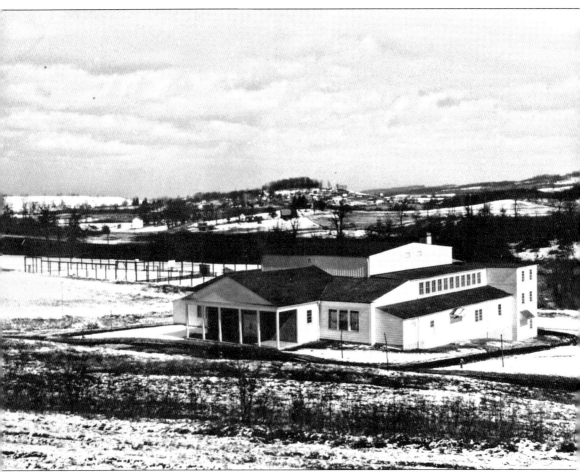

The center building, located between the high-school and elementary-school buildings, housed the cafeteria, kitchen, home-economics rooms, the community canning kitchen, the doctor's offices, the school bank, a bookstore, business and typing rooms, and the director's office. The Recreational Building, located adjacent to the high school, consisted of an auditorium/gymnasium that claimed to have the best basketball floor in the state, showers, dressing rooms, a stage, wings to allow for work on scenery and props, and an orchestra practice room. Clapp stated that the building embodied the "spirit of organized athletics" and was used after dark for activities, including volleyball and basketball. (Courtesy Library of Congress.)

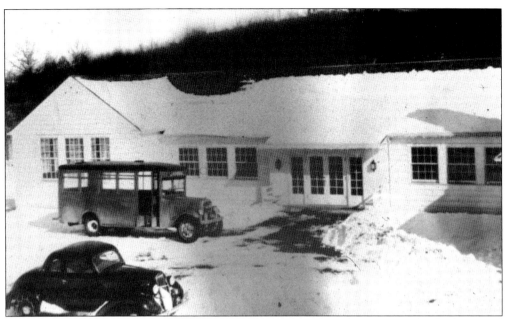

The new nursery school featured six large classrooms, each with its own toilet facilities and separate entrance to a playground. Sleeping porches were located at the rear of the building, extending into the playground to provide a shade on sunny days and a cover on rainy days. One-way observation windows were placed in several classrooms in order for visitors and mothers to observe the children without disrupting class. (Courtesy SCRC.)

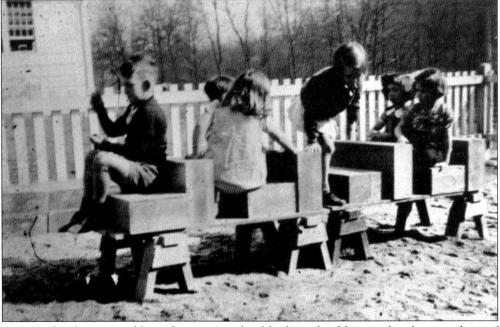

In 1935, the three year olds in the nursery school built a school bus on the playground out of planks, saw horses, and blocks. After building the bus, they put on a play and assumed the roles of teacher, bus driver, and students. Their bus was modeled after the bus the homesteaders rebuilt in order to provide transportation for the children to school. (Courtesy SCRC.)

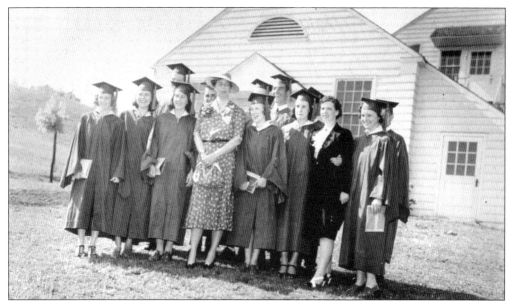

Clapp only served as administrator of the school until 1936, when it was turned over to the Preston County Board of Education. Eleanor Roosevelt continued to support the school financially, especially the nursery school, which could not receive state funds. She handed out diplomas at high-school graduations, invited classes to the White House for tea, and even helped graduates find jobs in Washington, D.C.

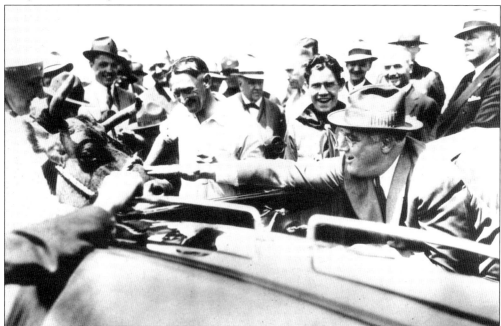

In 1938, the first lady sent a telegram to Arthurdale High School principal E. Grant Nine recommending the graduating class ask President Roosevelt to speak at their commencement ceremony. FDR accepted the invitation and visited Arthurdale for the first time in May 1938. Here Arthurdale homesteaders greet the president along with the community's prize cow, which he called a "West Virginia Moose." (Courtesy Franklin D. Roosevelt Library.)

$6.00 USD(includes any seller handling fees)

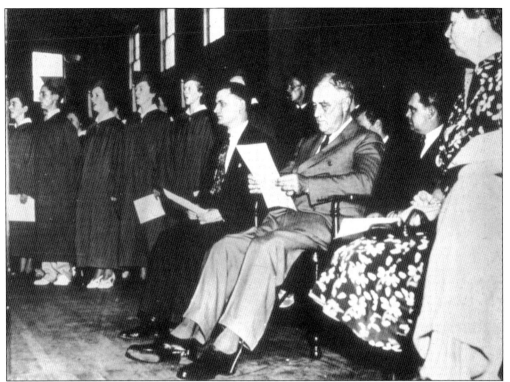

On May 27, 1938, Pres. Franklin D. Roosevelt gave the commencement address at the high-school graduation. The president stated that he could greet the residents of the community "as old friends because you are Mrs. Roosevelt's old friends and also because I have heard so much about you." This rare photograph shows the braces on the president's feet. (Courtesy WVRHC.)

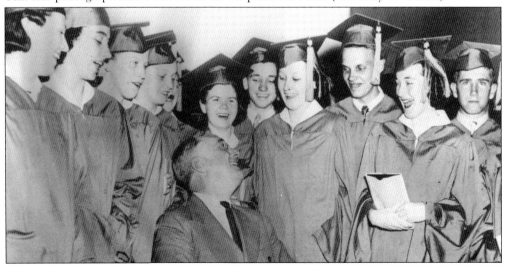

FDR spoke of the social responsibility through spending tax dollars and the imminent progressive tax law that was going into effect that night without his signature of approval. The president ended his speech by stating that he was "proud of what I have seen today and I am proud of all of you . . . who are helping so greatly to make this community an American success." (Courtesy Franklin D. Roosevelt Library, print obtained from WVRHC.)

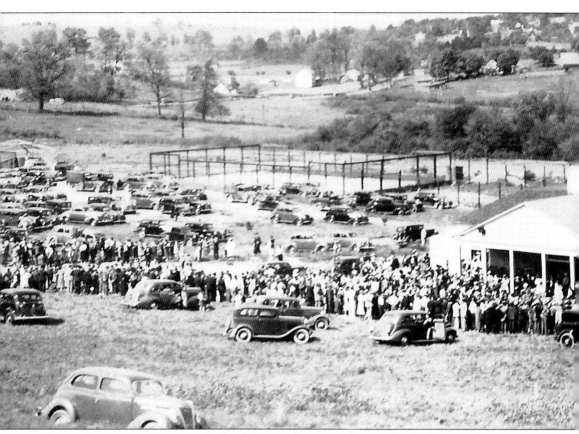

Secret Service agents came to Arthurdale a week prior to the president's visit in order to inspect roads, bridges, and culverts over which he would travel. The agents also went through the school buildings and inspected the list of food to be served on graduation day and where the food was going to be purchased. Two agents also remained in the kitchen during the entire preparation

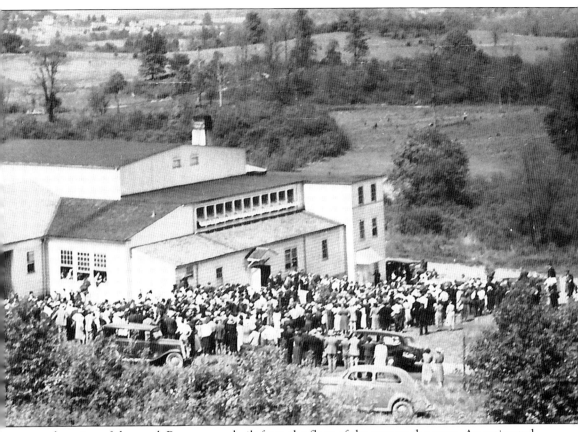

and serving of the meal. Ramps were built from the floor of the gym to the stage. An estimated 10,000 people came to the graduation ceremony. A loudspeaker was placed outside to allow everyone on the grounds to hear the president's speech. Newsreel cameras and radio stations could be found all around the building.

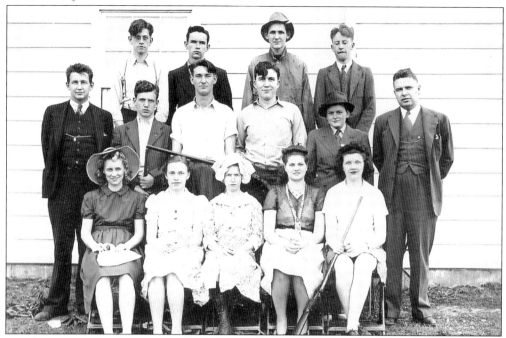

In order to raise money to travel to Washington, D.C., in the spring, the class of 1940 held two Victorian dances and sold candy. The remainder of the trip expenses was funded through the proceeds of the class play *Moonshine and Honeysuckle*, the cast of which is pictured. According to the 1940 yearbook, the class left on May 17 to "be guests of Mrs. Roosevelt at the White House."

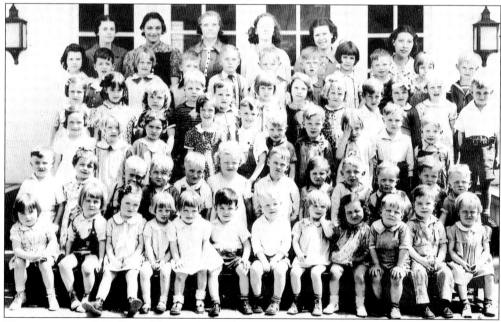

The new principal, E. Grant Nine, attempted to maintain Clapp's curriculum when he took over in 1936, but the board of education soon stopped funding what it considered special programs at Arthurdale. By World War II, the Arthurdale School was the same as other schools in Preston County. Arthurdale Primary School students from 1942–1943 are pictured here.

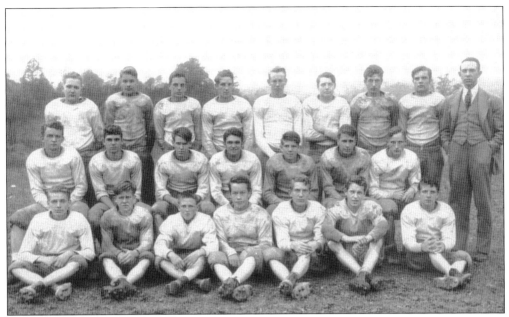

Because Arthurdale High School's enrollment was the smallest in the county, the school did not have enough students to support a regulation, 11-player football team. The team played six-man ball against competitors and was very successful throughout school history. Six-man football was developed during the Depression because of low school enrollment and is more fast-paced and played on a smaller football field. An early-1940s AHS football team is pictured.

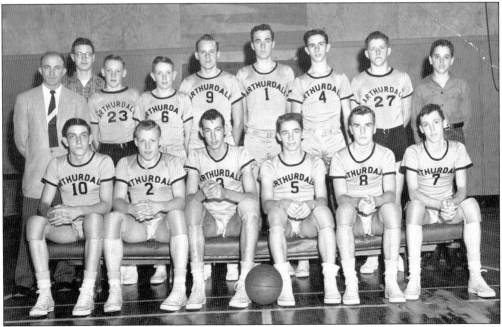

The 1955 basketball team was the only AHS team to make it to the regional tournament in school history. Although AHS was the smallest school in the county, the Pioneers won the sectional title and eventually met Aurora in the regional tournament. Although AHS lost in the championship game, the experience was one of the most memorable in school history.

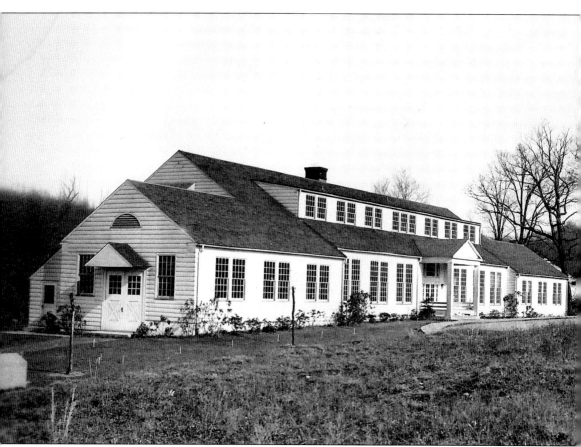

Although originally consisting of six buildings, the Arthurdale School lost two buildings to manufacturing operations during World War II. The nursery-school and primary-school buildings continued to be use as industrial centers until they were torn down. The Arthurdale High School, pictured in 1940, served as a community high school until 1956, when it was merged with Masontown High Schools to create Valley District High School. The four school buildings then served as a junior high and middle school until 1991. Valley Elementary resided in the Arthurdale School buildings until 2000. At that time, Preston County Board of Education transferred the high school, center building, and elementary school to Arthurdale Heritage. The gym where President Roosevelt gave the 1938 graduation commencement address continues to be used by Valley Elementary School.

Eight

ELEANOR'S LITTLE VILLAGE

Born in 1884 to a socially prestigious family in New York, Anna Eleanor Roosevelt lived her life as a true philanthropist. She became interested in social issues while studying in England under Marie Souvestre at the beginning of the 20th century. Upon her return to the United States, Eleanor began working in a settlement house, much to her Grandmother Hall's chagrin. Eleanor found her humanitarian instincts from the Roosevelts, who, she said, were "not so much concerned with Society as with people, and these people included the newsboys from the streets of New York and cripples."

She married Franklin Delano Roosevelt in 1905 and put aside her charitable work while he pursued his political career. She returned to social activism shortly after World War I when she discovered FDR had been having an affair with her social secretary, Lucy Mercer. Yet when FDR contracted polio, Eleanor became his face in public, making speeches on social reform in his name. She became a staunch women's activist, a skilled public speaker, and a writer for national publications.

In 1933, Eleanor made a commitment to the people of Scotts Run to help them through the harsh economic period through which they were living. She took it upon herself to make Arthurdale a project that would be beneficial to the downtrodden coal miners of West Virginia and argued against the Communistic label that had been put on it stating, "[n]ever in this country to my knowledge has it been considered communistic for an opportunity to be given to people to earn their own livings and buy their own homes." According to the first lady, Arthurdale represented how people in America had a right to live. In her eyes, the project was a future of dignity for every family in the community through a "program of long time rehabilitation."

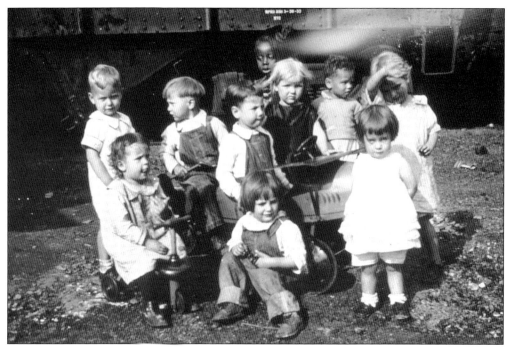

When the first lady visited Scotts Run and saw the meager conditions in which children were living, she began to fight for its residents, who, she believed, had a right to receive "a minimum of security and happiness in life. They must have enough to eat, warmth, adequate clothing, decent shelter, and an opportunity for education." (Courtesy WVRHC.)

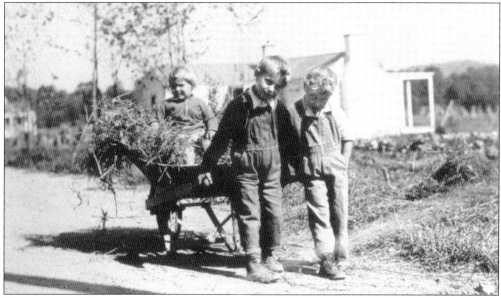

Eleanor Roosevelt saw an opportunity in Arthurdale to create a truly cooperative community, with neighbors helping neighbors in all respects. "Communities of this type presuppose that the people living in them are going to be interested in the welfare of the whole community and that they are going to be . . . less selfish and more willing to share their security with those around them." (Courtesy Library of Congress.)

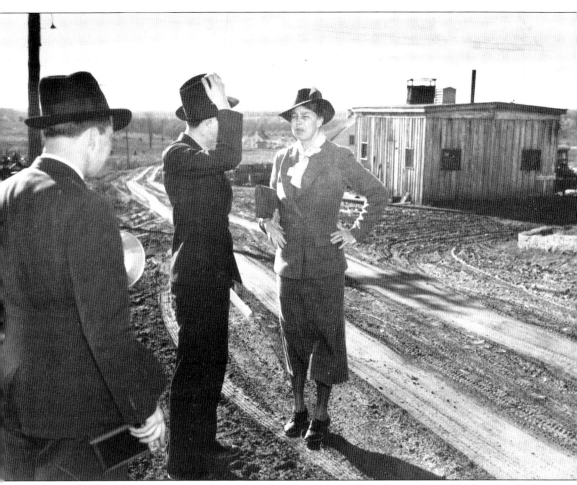

Eleanor lobbied for electricity, appliances, and bathrooms in all the homes. Harold Ickes, head of the Department of the Interior, complained to FDR about the money being spent in Arthurdale, stating the project worried him more than any other project in his department. With all the amenities being provided to the homesteaders, Ickes asked how one would be able to tell the rich from the poor. Eleanor Roosevelt replied that in matters of simple dignity and decency, one should not be able to tell the rich from the poor. Ickes continued to complain to the president, to which FDR replied, "My Missus, unlike most women, hasn't any sense about money at all." (Courtesy WVRHC.)

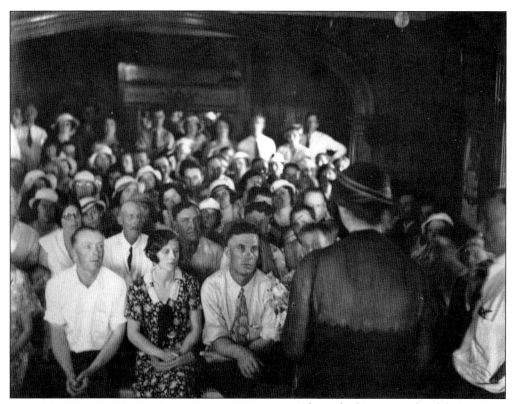

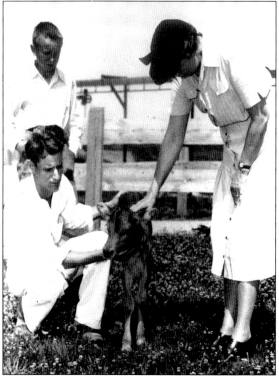

Always looking at Arthurdale in a positive light, Eleanor supported it as an experimental project, stating that its blunders would be beneficial to other projects in the future. If the Hodgson homes had not been tried in Arthurdale, they would have in another community. The first lady did not approve of the non-experimental way the homesteaders were chosen, saying it was unwise to "hand pick the tenants because again I feel that it must be an experiment in ordinary life and an ordinary community contains people of every type and ability and character." However, she continued to support Arthurdale with the thought that "many human beings who might have cost us thousands of dollars in tuberculosis sanitariums, insane asylums, and jails were restored to usefulness and given confidence in themselves." (Above courtesy WVRHC; below courtesy Franklin D. Roosevelt Library.)

Eleanor Roosevelt's presence brought numerous media outlets to Arthurdale. She wrote about Arthurdale in her national columns, during lectures, in women's magazines, and on her radio show. All her earnings as a result of this publicity were donated to charity, including to Arthurdale, through the American Friends Service Committee. (Courtesy Franklin D. Roosevelt Library.)

The first lady donated $36,000 to the Friends in 1934 alone, and the money was spent on teachers' salaries, school supplies, and equipment in Arthurdale. She also brought wealthy citizens such as tobacco heiress Doris Duke, pictured behind Roosevelt, to Arthurdale and other homestead communities, hoping to persuade them to donate money to the projects. (Courtesy WVRHC.)

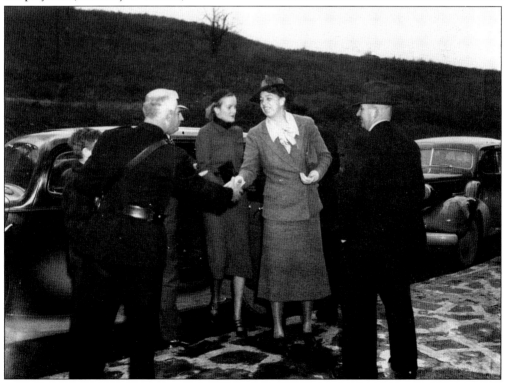

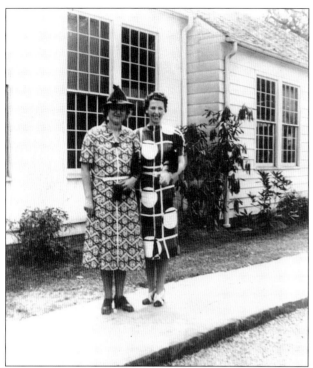

After an Arthurdale teacher told the first lady about the school not having enough money to buy books, Eleanor Roosevelt came to Arthurdale with Elinor Morgenthau, wife of the Secretary of the Treasury Henry Morgenthau. The Morgenthaus donated $1,000 to buy books and sent furniture for the library. Morgenthau is pictured on the left with an Arthurdale School teacher. (Courtesy WVRHC.)

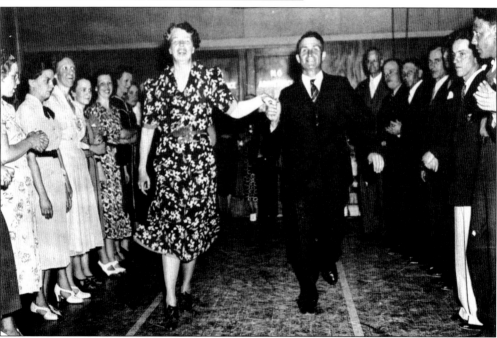

A former Arthurdale School teacher remembered the first lady as "such as pleasant person. She acted as if she had known you all your life. . . . She just felt like she was one of us." Eleanor Roosevelt loved to square dance and during her visits to Arthurdale could be found dancing her favorite dance, the Virginia Reel, with homesteaders on Saturday night. (Courtesy Franklin D. Roosevelt Library, print obtained from WVRHC.)

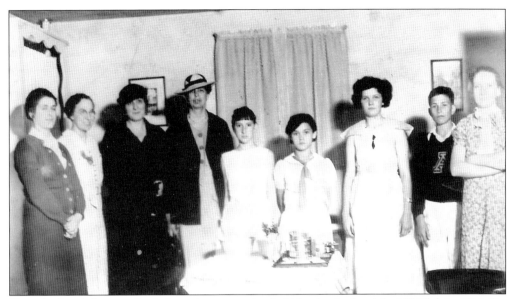

Here the first lady attends a baking demonstration held by the Arthurdale 4-H Club in 1936. On the same trip, she attended the dedication of the vacuum factory and the high-school graduation, and handed out winning ribbons at the music festival. It was not uncommon for her to also visit individual homesteads to inquire how they were doing, what they might need, and how she could help.

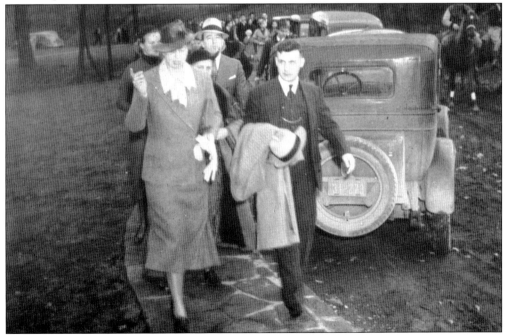

Roosevelt believed that through education, "[M]en and women will finally learn how to live happily and securely together. . . . They will develop in an economy of peace and plenty rather than competition and want." She is pictured here with E. Grant Nine, who took over as principal of the school after Clapp left. Doris Duke and Jennings Randolph are pictured behind them. (Courtesy WVRHC.)

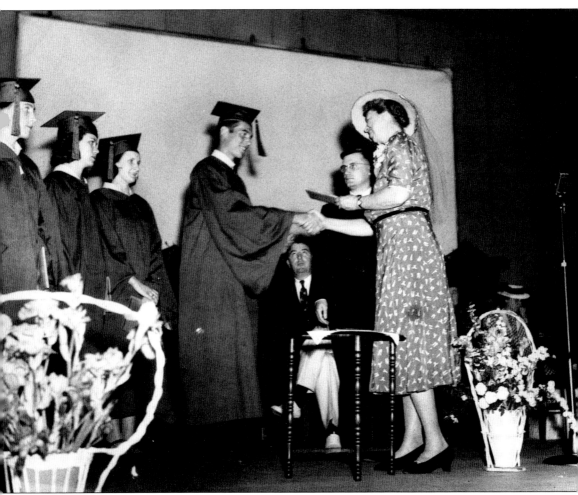

It became customary for high-school graduating classes to invite the first lady to their graduation ceremony and present her with flowers. She spoke at and handed out diplomas at every graduation from 1935 to 1944. When she handed out diplomas at the 1939 class graduation pictured here, Roosevelt observed that the students were "all well fed and they looked healthy." (Courtesy WVRHC.)

Nine
THE DREAM LIVES ON

As early as 1938, congressional support of the homestead program began to diminish. Despite the lack of support, the Farm Security Administration, the third of the federal agencies to oversee Arthurdale, refused to sell off the homes and property due to the homesteaders' lack of income. Without a steady source of employment, the homesteaders would not be able to purchase their homesteads. The attack on the homestead program became more elevated in the 1940s when Congress forbade additional expenditures. By 1941, plans were under way to liquidate Arthurdale.

Milford Mott was hired as community manager to execute the final sale of all the government holdings in the community. The first homestead sales were based on income and fair evaluation with no down payment required. Although the fair market value of the homes was approximately $6,000, they only sold from $750 to $1,249. Arthurdale and other non-farming communities were transferred to the Federal Public Housing Authority in 1942, which raised the prices on homesteads not already under contract. All homesteads were sold by 1947.

For 40 years, Arthurdale operated as any other community in West Virginia. The center-complex buildings changed owners, were subject to a fire in the 1970s, and by 1984, sat in a deteriorated state, unused by the public. That same year, community members organized an event to celebrate the 50th anniversary of Arthurdale's homesteading. Titled "The Arthurdale Dream Then and Now," the celebration featured exhibits, tours, and dances at the Arthurdale School buildings, where community members reminisced about the community's rich history and how their dreams became a reality in 1934.

Arthurdale Heritage, Inc., was formed in 1985 as a result of this celebration. Arthurdale Heritage is a nonprofit organization dedicated to the preservation of historic Arthurdale, and it operates the New Deal Homestead Museum as a living proof of the social success of the community and homestead program.

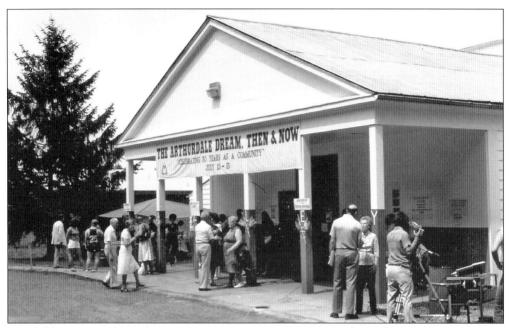

Funded by a grant from the West Virginia Humanities Council, residents from Arthurdale organized a weekend of festivities that celebrated the 50th Anniversary of the homesteading of Arthurdale. The celebration took place July 13 through 15, 1984, at the Arthurdale School buildings. As a result of this celebration, Arthurdale Heritage, Inc., was chartered as a nonprofit organization in October 1985.

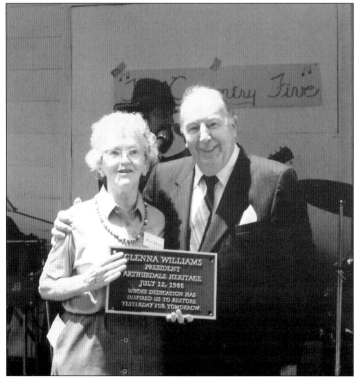

Arthurdale Heritage held its first homecoming in July 1986. The event included historic photograph displays in the administration building, music, and a craft market. Arthurdale Heritage's first president, Glenna Williams is pictured with Sen. Jennings Randolph, who was the celebration's honored guest. Randolph reminisced about his connection with Arthurdale's formative years and stated how proud he was to be a part of its restoration.

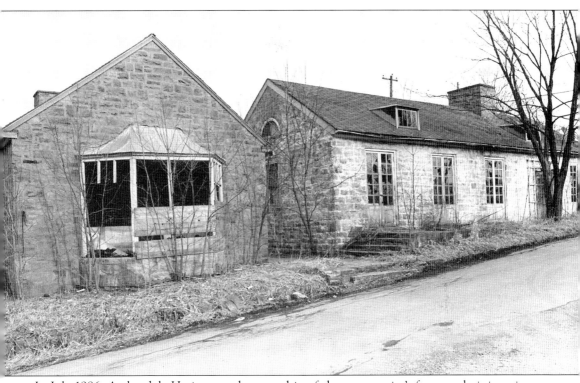

In July 1986, Arthurdale Heritage took ownership of the community's former administration building (right), Forge (left), and service station from Ralph Brown. Brown had purchased the buildings in 1952 and operated the service station as a family business until 1960. His decision to sell the buildings to Arthurdale Heritage made a substantial contribution to the organization's initial success. "I could have sold the property for more money," Brown said, "but I wanted a group such as AH to have it because the Arthurdale community has been good to my family. I feel I am paying back some of the contribution paid to my life." Despite sitting vacant for decades, the buildings still showed glimpses of their former stateliness. Arthurdale Heritage volunteers began work on June 14, 1986, to clean up the buildings.

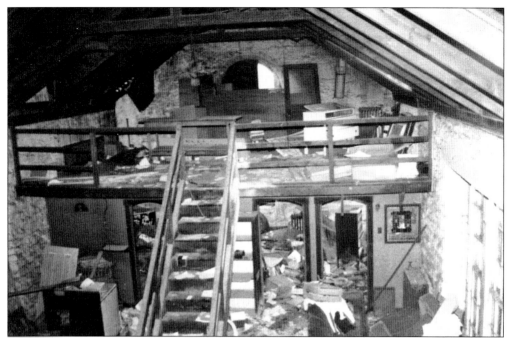

The administration building had been used as a storage unit. Volunteers removed truckloads of debris from the building. Brush and undergrowth were also cut away from the buildings. Volunteers eventually put a new roof on the building in 1988. That same year, Arthurdale Heritage burned the mortgage on the Brown Property.

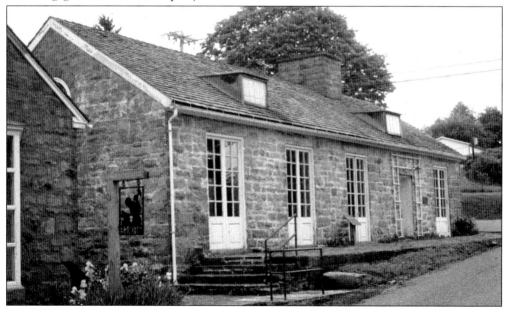

Arthurdale Heritage opened a visitor center on weekends in July and August 1991 in the administration building. In the 1990s, the building housed the visitor center, museum, and offices, while other center-complex buildings were being restored. Currently the administration building is one of five buildings that make up the New Deal Homestead Museum, which is open year-round.

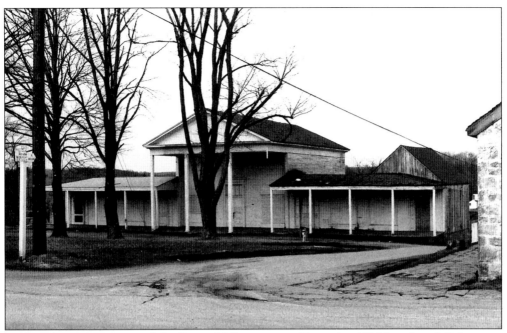

Arthurdale Heritage acquired the Center Hall property in November 1986 from Joseph Belmaggio, who also donated $5,000 toward its preservation. The right wing of the center was restored in 1992 with funds from the Claude Worthington Benedum Foundation. The remainder of the building was restored in 1995 through a Housing and Urban Development grant.

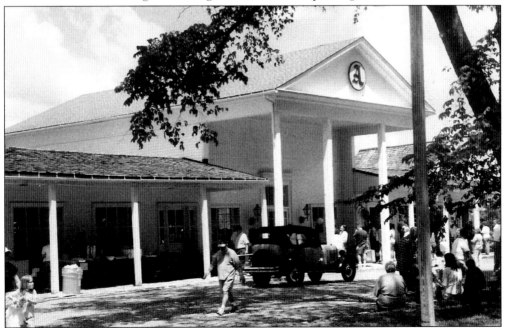

The Arthurdale Heritage Craft Shop opened in the former MCCA Craft Shop in 1999, and the Arthurdale Heritage Visitor Center moved to the Center Hall in 2001. The building has once again become the center for community activity where square dances, dance classes, and dinners are held. A scene from the 2001 New Deal Festival is pictured.

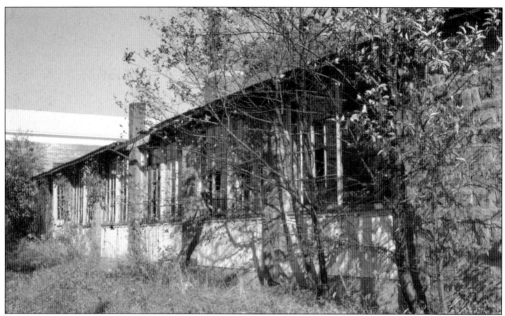

In the spring of 1987, Arthurdale Heritage acquired the Blake property, which included the former Mountaineer Craftmen's furniture factory shops, the general store, and weaving room. A fire destroyed the general store and weaving room in the 1970s. The remains of the furniture workshops are pictured in 1987. Volunteers began cleaning up the property by removing unstable structures.

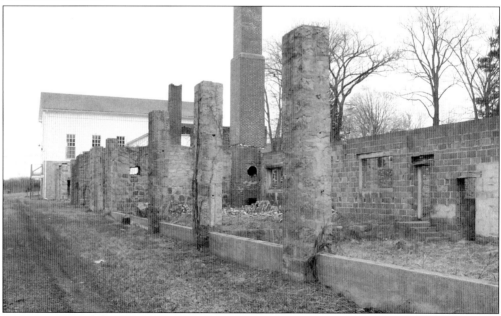

In 1991, Arthurdale Heritage burned the final mortgage on the Blake property, making the organization debt free. Arthurdale Heritage has made rebuilding the South Side structures one of its goals, which when achieved, will complete the restoration of the original Arthurdale community-center complex. Currently only the stone piers, some cinder block walls, and two chimneys from the steam plant are all that remain of the complex.

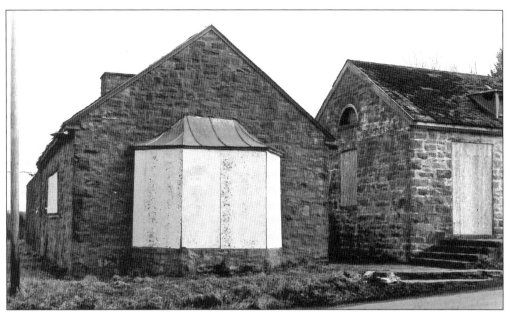

In 1989, Arthurdale Heritage received a grant from the West Virginia State Historic Preservation office to restore the Forge. Volunteers logged 870 hours of work building a new roof, rebuilding the bay window, and restoring the interior to a working forge. That same year, Arthurdale was placed on the National Register of Historic Places as a 1,000-acre historic district, and Arthurdale Heritage received the Albert B. Corey Award from the American Association of State and Local History for excellence in volunteerism. In 1994, Arthurdale Heritage celebrated the 60th anniversary of the homesteading of Arthurdale through historic displays, a craft sale, tours of the Arthurdale School buildings, and Arthurdale homestead tours. The organization also hosted "A New Deal for America," a national conference at which speakers discussed Scotts Run, the Arthurdale School system, Eleanor Roosevelt, and the subsistence homestead program.

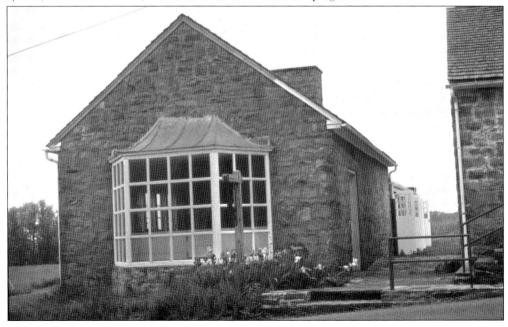

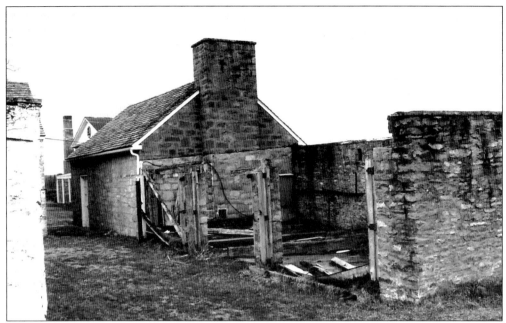

In 1992 and 1995, Arthurdale Heritage received two Housing and Urban Development grants totaling $800,000 to restore the Center Hall, garage bays, and Esso Station. As pictured, the garage bays behind the Forge and in between the service station and administration building had to be completely rebuilt. The bays originally served as storage, housed federal automobiles, and were work areas for the service station.

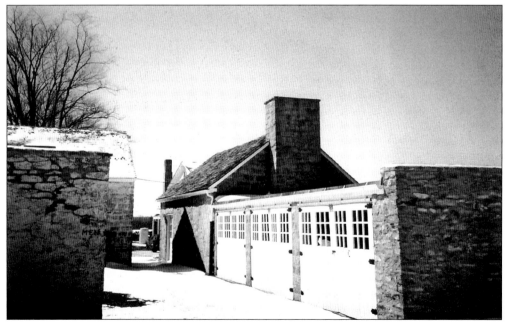

The restored Esso Station opened in 1995 with the help of the local antique car club, the Arthurdale Tire Kickers. In 2001, the club donated various Esso items, which are on display inside the service station, and has installed an old Esso sign and antique gasoline pumps that advertise gasoline for sale at 17¢ a gallon.

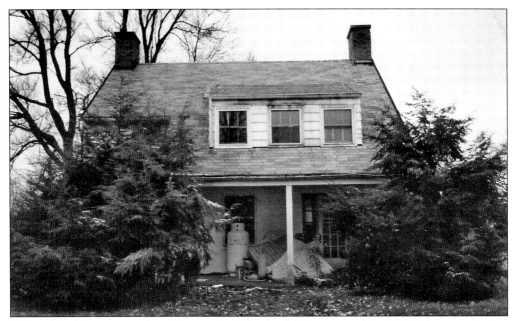

Arthurdale Heritage purchased an original Arthurdale homestead in 1998. The organization used remaining funds from its Housing and Urban Development grant and raised an additional $15,000 in less than 45 days to purchase the house and property. The ribbon-cutting ceremony for the E-15 Homestead was held on June 5, 1999, complete with Arthurdale "homesteaders," as portrayed by living history actors.

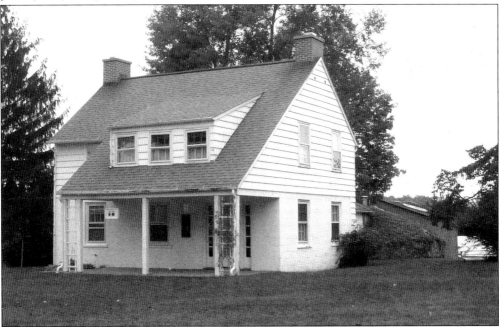

A Wagner home, the E-15 Homestead, is part of the New Deal Homestead Museum and gives visitors to Arthurdale a glimpse of what life was like in the 1930s for homesteaders. Annually, Arthurdale Heritage hosts the New Deal Festival, which celebrates not only the history of Arthurdale, but also the legacy of Franklin D. Roosevelt's legislation.

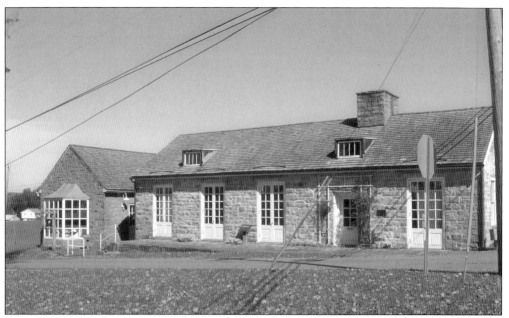

After 20 years of operation, Arthurdale Heritage owns eight historic buildings on 24 acres of property, has received over $1.6 million in grant money, and has amassed countless hours of volunteer service. The organization continues to follow its mission of preserving historic Arthurdale, and its New Deal Homestead Museum serves as a living testament to the life-altering homestead program.

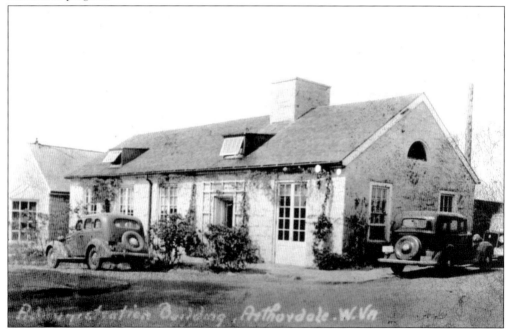

Arthurdale Heritage strives to present historic Arthurdale as a continuing legacy of the remarkable work completed by former First Lady Eleanor Roosevelt. As the public becomes more intrigued with this wonderful story, the spirit of the 1930s is returning to Arthurdale and visitors are once again coming to see "Eleanor's Little Village." (Courtesy WVRHC.)

BIBLIOGRAPHY

Anderson, Colleen. "Arthurdale Craftspeople, 1974." *Goldenseal*. Vol. 7, Issue 2: 21–25.

Clapp, Elsie Ripley. *Community Schools in Action*. New York: Viking Press, 1939.

Cook, Blanche Wiesen. *Eleanor Roosevelt, Vol. II: 1933–1938*. New York: Viking Penguin, 1999.

Conkin, Paul. *Tomorrow a New World: The New Deal Community Program*. New York: Cornell UP, 1959.

Cullinan, Kathleen and Beth Spence. "Arthurdale: The New Deal Comes to Preston County." *Goldenseal*. Vol. 7, Issue 2: 7-20.

Haid, Stephen. "Arthurdale: An Experiment in Community Planning, 1933–1947." Ph.D. diss. West Virginia University, 1975.

Kreiser, Christine M., ed. "'I Wonder whom God will hold responsible: Mary Behner and the Presbyterian Mission on Scotts Run." *West Virginia History*. Vol. 53, 1994: 61–94.

Lewis, Ronald. "Scotts Run: An Introduction." *West Virginia History*. Vol. 53, 1994: 1–6.

Maxwell, John. "'Learning by Doing': Teachers Remember Arthurdale School." *Goldenseal*. Vol. 8, Issue 1: 65–71.

Preston County, West Virginia. US: Taylor Publishing Company, 1979.

Roosevelt, Eleanor. *This I Remember*. New York: Harper & Brothers, 1949.

Rymer, Jeanne S. "Arthurdale, a Social Experiment in the 1930s: Foundations, Fantasies, Furniture, and Failures." *West Virginia History*. Vol. 46, 1985–1986.

Stack, Sam F., Jr. *Elsie Ripley Clapp (1879–1965): Her Life and The Community School*. New York: Peter Lang, 2004.

Thomas, Jerry Bruce. *An Appalachian New Deal: West Virginia in the Great Depression*. Kentucky: University of Kentucky, 1998.

Ward, Bryan, ed. *A New Deal For America*. Arthurdale: Arthurdale Heritage, Inc., 1995.

ACROSS AMERICA, PEOPLE ARE DISCOVERING
SOMETHING WONDERFUL. *THEIR HERITAGE.*

Arcadia Publishing is the leading local history publisher in the United States. With more than 3,000 titles in print and hundreds of new titles released every year, Arcadia has extensive specialized experience chronicling the history of communities and celebrating America's hidden stories, bringing to life the people, places, and events from the past. To discover the history of other communities across the nation, please visit:

www.arcadiapublishing.com

Customized search tools allow you to find regional history books about the town where you grew up, the cities where your friends and family live, the town where your parents met, or even that retirement spot you've been dreaming about.

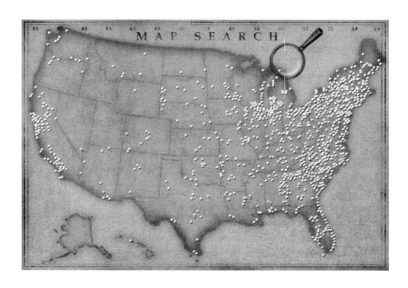